·KIDSWORKS·

Creative Crafts for Clever Kids

Written by Loralyn Radcliffe

Illustrations by Barb Lorseyedi

Teacher Created Materials

Teacher Created Materials, Inc.
P.O. Box 1040
Huntington Beach, CA 92647
©1996 Teacher Created Materials, Inc.
Made in U.S.A.

ISBN #1-55734-678-X

Library of Congress Catalog Card Number: 95-62417

Editor:
Marsha Kearns

Table of Contents

Table of Contents (cont.)

Introduction

Welcome to **Creative Crafts for Clever Kids**!

The exciting projects in this 160-page book will provide your children with many happy hours of creative activity. "Materials" lists everything necessary to complete the project. The main craft ideas are extended with "More Ideas," which offers alternatives for decorating and using the completed projects and for creating different ones.

Most materials are readily available from hobby shops, hardware and fabric stores, or your local grocery. You may find some of the materials in your home—or even in your own backyard. Don't be afraid to substitute if you think something else may work instead of—or better than—what is suggested. The emphasis here is on being creative.

For your convenience, the crafts are divided into sections according to the main type of material used.

- **Paper Productions:** Create from paper products such wonders as a rocking horse, newspaper fan, portfolio, building logs, and jewelry.

- **Kitchen Capers:** Use everyday food items to craft interesting items such as a potato hedgehog, sugar cube igloo, candy-cup magnet, colored rice mosaic, and apple votive candle.

- **Natural Necessities:** Things found in nature yield a surprising variety of treasures such as nuthead magnets, dandelion jewelry, mud building bricks, and "pet" rocks that double as game pieces.

- **Clay Dough Creations:** This section provides recipes for four different kinds of clay dough, followed by a selection of creative clay crafts such as birthday candle holders, potted plant people, beautiful beads, dinosaur teeth, jewelry, and woven baskets.

- **Fabric Finery:** Your children will marvel as they use such materials as fabric, ribbon, felt, and yarn to make dolls, flowers, picture frames, hats, and indoor tennis rackets.

- **Hardware Handiwork:** Leftover nuts, bolts, washers, cans, and cup hooks turn from nuisances into neat stuff such as jewelry, wind chimes, animals, and sculpture.

- **Trash Treasures:** Create environmentally friendly crafts by cleaning and reusing such materials as cans, milk jugs, egg cartons, plastic six-pack rings, and soda bottles.

How to Use This Book

Preview the Book: Page through the book to familiarize yourself with the types of crafts and the layout of the craft sections. Artwork showing some projects is included to help clarify the instructions. In addition, the more difficult steps are also illustrated.

Gathering Materials: Note things you can begin to collect and recycle as you go about your daily activities. These could include things found in the home, such as plastic bottles, jugs, and six-pack rings; different sizes of cans; foam egg cartons and meat trays; and bits of fabric, ribbon, and string. Or you may find things in nature, such as feathers, nuts, rocks, seeds, and leaves. There may be still other items—such as craft sticks, construction paper, scissors, tape, glue, paint, brushes, markers, and crayons—that you will want to purchase to keep on hand.

Storing Materials: Set aside a shelf, drawer, or container that will serve as a permanent place to store all craft materials. Make the storage place accessible to your children so they can contribute to the collectibles whenever they find something they think would be fun to use. Remind kids to respect others by asking before they take anything that is not theirs. This includes items in nature that are homes to animals. Tell children to check with you before they take something from the environment.

Getting Started: Help children get started by reading aloud together the directions and talking about the craft they have chosen. Be sure to check the "Materials" section to ensure you have the necessary materials to complete a chosen project. The clay crafts may involve two steps: following the recipe to make the clay, and then completing the craft idea. Perhaps you will make the clay one day and use it for crafting on another day. Older kids will probably be able to complete most of the crafts with only a little help. Younger children may need further assistance assembling the materials and following the directions.

Safety Concerns: Remember to read the "Safety Guidelines" on page 7 before each craft session to minimize the risk of accidents. Make sure you note the projects that require your continued active involvement because of safety concerns or difficulty. Guide children to choose crafts that are appropriate for the amount of time you have available.

Encouraging Creativity: You may be tempted to do things yourself, but be patient and remember that these are your children's creations. Contribute only what is necessary for your kids to proceed, and be ready to rave about the results—no matter what they look like! With this book—and a little planning—you will always have a ready answer when your kids say, "I'm bored. What can I do?"

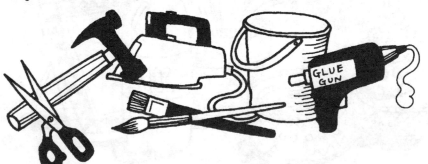

Safety Guidelines

For Adults

1. Remember to read the directions completely and carefully before you help your children start a project.

2. Actively assist with the crafts that need adult supervision for safety—those that require use of an iron, stove, hot-glue gun, tools, or sharp utensils.

3. Thoroughly clean all previously used containers. Add a little chlorine bleach to the cleaning water to kill bacteria.

4. Never use meat trays that have held raw chicken. Egg shells should be rinsed inside and out with chlorine bleach to destroy potentially dangerous bacteria.

5. Cover work surfaces with a protective layer of cloth, plastic, cardboard, or newspaper.

6. Parcel out small items such as buttons and seeds one at a time to younger children. Be sure to stress that these items should never be put in their mouths.

7. Model "safety first" behavior as you work with your children. When you are through using a potentially dangerous implement, put it away, turn it off, or otherwise secure it to prevent injury.

8. Teach children to clean up and put things away in their proper places after completing the activity.

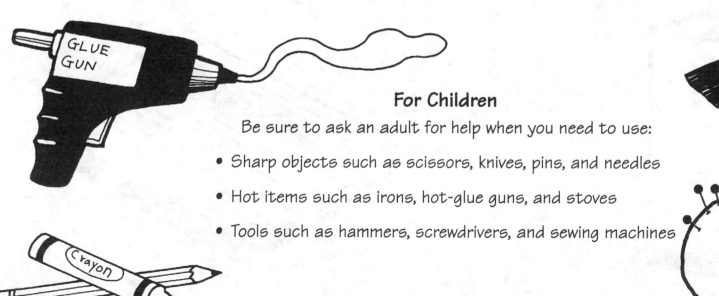

For Children

Be sure to ask an adult for help when you need to use:

- Sharp objects such as scissors, knives, pins, and needles

- Hot items such as irons, hot-glue guns, and stoves

- Tools such as hammers, screwdrivers, and sewing machines

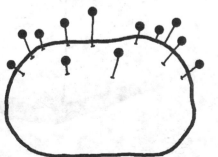

Paper Productions

Computer Paper Creature

- Newspaper
- String or yarn
- Computer paper tear-off edge strips
- Glue
- Scissors
- Crayons or markers
- Construction paper

1. Roll up a sheet of newspaper. Tie each end of the roll with string or yarn to form a creature's body.

2. Draw or glue on facial features to the center of the newspaper body.

3. Glue computer-paper edge strips to the creature to form tentacles.

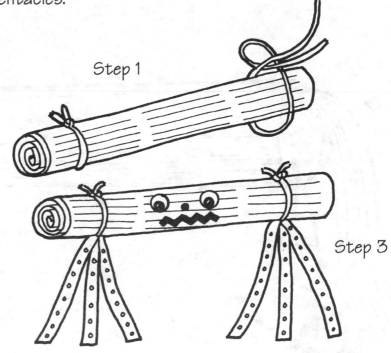

Step 1

Step 3

MORE IDEAS

- Attach a string to both ends of the creature and hang it from your ceiling.
- Turn the newspaper body on end. Glue the computer-paper edge strips to the top of the body to create a mop of wild hair. Add facial features.
- Tie a string around the middle of a mass of edge strips to make a multilegged spider. Hang it from your ceiling.

Rocking Horse

It Really Rocks!

Rocking Horse

- Paper plate
- Toilet paper tube
- Construction paper
- Yarn
- Scissors
- Glue
- Crayons or markers

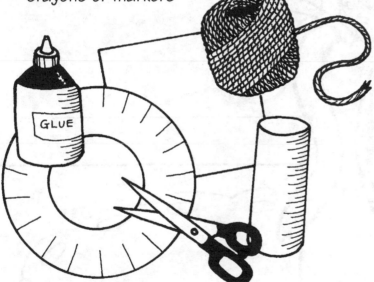

1. Fold the paper plate in half.
2. Cut the toilet paper tube from end to end. Slide the folded side of the paper plate into the slit in the tube. Glue the tube to the paper plate.
3. Fold the construction paper in half. Cut out the shape of a horse's neck and head, leaving the fold along the top of its nose. Draw on facial features with markers or crayons.
4. Open the head/neck piece and glue the neck ends to the sides of the tube. Add a yarn mane and tail.
5. Spread the edges of the paper plate to form the rocker.

Step 2

Step 3

MORE IDEAS

- Create different rocking animals by cutting out and adding different heads and features.
- Make animals that stand rather than rock. Leave the tube uncut. Insert bundles of four toothpicks, wrapped with rubber bands, for legs.
- Add a construction paper saddle and bridle.

Envelope Bags

Use These Bags to Hold Your Tiny Treasures

12

Envelope Bags

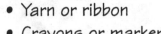

MATERIALS

- Envelope, any size or color (makes 2 bags)
- Scissors
- Glue or tape
- Hole punch
- Yarn or ribbon
- Crayons or markers

LET'S DO IT!!

1. Seal the envelope and then cut it in half widthwise.
2. Fold the uncut edges in about ¾" (2 cm), creasing them well.
3. Open one half, place your hand inside, and reverse the folds to the inside.
4. Tape or glue the corner triangular flaps to the bottom of the bag.
5. Punch holes on the sides to tie on yarn or ribbon for a handle and decorate your bags.

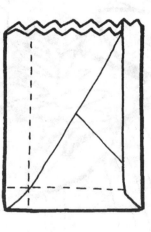

Step 2

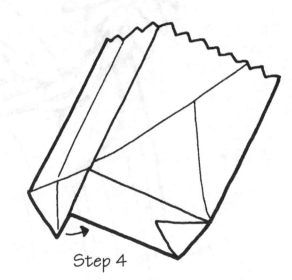

Step 4

MORE IDEAS

- Use pipe cleaners for handles.
- Cut the envelope in half with decorative-cut scissors for a fancy top edge.
- Use the bags to hold your treasures or as party favors.

Colorful Flower Wreath

Prettier Than a Hat!

14

Colorful Flower Wreath

- Tissue paper or crepe paper streamer
- Scissors
- Green pipe cleaners
- Green construction paper
- Glue

1. Cut the tissue paper into strips 1 ½" x 15" (3.74 cm x 37.5 cm).

2. Glue one short end of the strip to the end of a pipe cleaner. Wind the strip around the pipe cleaner, gluing it as you go. Pinch the base of the flower to shape it and secure it to the pipe cleaner.

3. Make ½" (1.3 cm) slits in the top of the tissue paper. Fluff out the petals.

4. Make several flowers. Cut off the excess pipe cleaner, leaving a ½" (1.3 cm) stem.

5. Twist pipe cleaners together to make a wreath to fit your head. Twist the stems of the flowers onto the wreath. Fill in the spaces with green construction paper leaves.

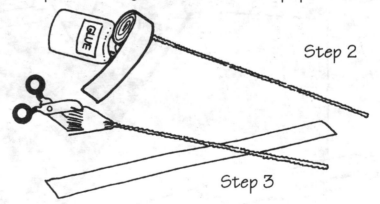

Step 2

Step 3

MORE IDEAS

- Make flowers from several different colors of tissue paper to create a more colorful wreath.
- Make two-colored flowers by wrapping and gluing an 8" (24 cm) length of the first color around a pipe cleaner, followed by an 8" (24 cm) length of the second color.
- Leave the stems long and arrange the individual flowers in a vase.

Marbleized Portfolio

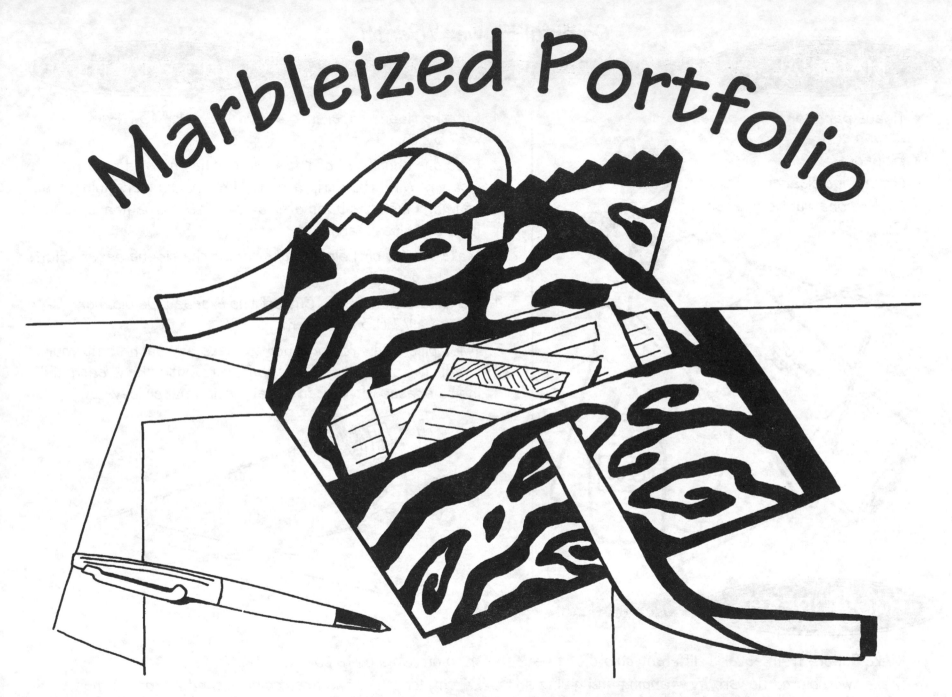

Store Your Important Papers in This Pretty Portfolio

Marbleized Portfolio

MATERIALS

- 12" x 20" (30 cm x 51 cm) piece of construction paper
- Two pieces of ribbon, 12" (30 cm) long
- Assorted colors of spray paint or oil-base paint
- Dishpan of cold water
- Scissors
- Glue
- Ruler
- Pencil
- Tape

LET'S DO IT!!

1. Marbleize the paper by spraying the water with paint, swirling the colors together, and laying the paper on the water. Remove the paper and let it dry.

2. Create flaps by drawing a light line 5" (12.5 cm) across one short end of the paper and 6" (15.25 cm) across the other short end. Fold along the lines.

3. Open the flaps. Trim ½" (1.3 cm) off sides, starting at 6" flap and ending at 5" fold line.

4. Fold inside tabs on 5" flap, fold up flap, and glue tabs to midsection.

5. Cut slits in the top and bottom flaps, insert the ends of the ribbons, and glue the ends to the underside. Tie ribbons to close the portfolio.

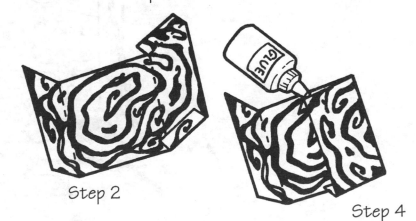

Step 2

Step 4

MORE IDEAS

- Decorate the portfolio using crayons, markers, stickers, or glitter.
- Make a decorative edge by cutting the top flap with decorative-cut scissors.
- Instead of marbleizing the portfolio, spatter-paint it. Dip an old toothbrush into paint. Point the bristle end of the toothbrush toward the portfolio. Run your thumb along the bristles to spatter the paint onto the portfolio.

Stage Necklace

Always Have a Puppet Stage Ready to Use

Stage Necklace

- One letter size file folder
- Scissors
- Ruler
- Hole punch
- Crayons or markers
- Yarn

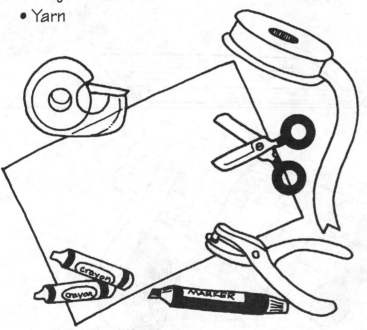

1. Cut out the center of one of the sides of a folder leaving a one-inch border. (This will look like a frame.)
2. On the side opposite the frame draw a scene. The bottom of the scene should end at the fold. This will serve as the background for the stage.
3. Punch holes in all four corners of the file folder. Thread yarn through the holes leaving enough to open the stage while suspended around your neck. See illustration. Tie the yarn into a knot.

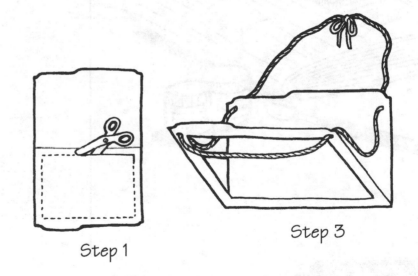

Step 1

Step 3

MORE IDEAS

- Make your fingers into puppets by drawing on faces and hair.
- Use the stage with glove puppets (see page 112).
- Instead of drawing a scene, tape a photograph of a landscape onto the backdrop.

Newspaper Log Construction

MATERIALS

- Newspaper
- Masking tape
- Scissors
- Paints
- Paintbrush

LET'S DO IT!!

1. Roll a sheet of newspaper tightly into a log and tape it shut.
2. Create many logs of varying sizes.
3. Use tape to lash the logs together to create a structure.
4. Paint your structure.

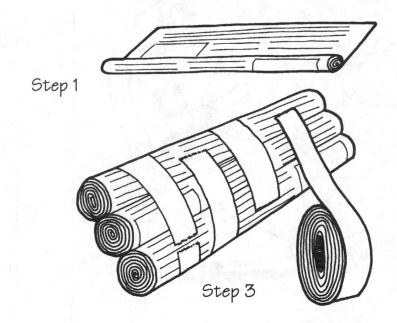

Step 1

Step 3

MORE IDEAS

- Use brown construction paper for logs.
- Create a bridge, tower, log cabin, or doll chair.
- Use string to lash logs together so you can reuse the logs.

Pine Tree

- Paper towel tube
- Construction paper
- Gift wrap strips, 3" (7.5 cm) wide
- Tape
- Glue
- Scissors

1. Roll a piece of construction paper into a cone shape and tape the edges to secure the cone.

2. Apply glue liberally to one end of the tube. Push the glued end of the tube into the cone and let it dry.

3. Cut 2" (5 cm) slits in the gift wrap strips ¼" (0.6 cm) apart to make fringed pieces.

4. Curl the fringe and glue the pieces to the cone. Start at the bottom and work to the top, overlapping the pieces of fringe so the cone doesn't show.

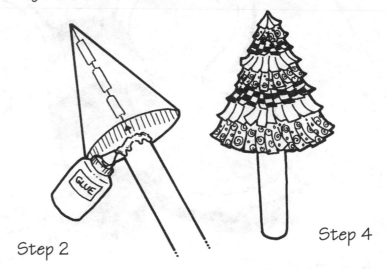

Step 2

Step 4

MORE IDEAS

- Make smaller trees by using a toilet paper tube and shorter paper fringe.
- Use the trees around your pretzel log cabin (see page 38).
- Create a forest centerpiece: Make trees of varying heights and glue them to a cardboard base. Glue small leaves and twigs to the base. Make clay animals to hide among the trees.

Paper Pin-On Jewelry

Paper Jewelry Is Easy to Make and Fun to Wear

Paper Pin-On Jewelry

- Watercolor paper
- Crayons, colored pencils, or permanent markers
- Black permanent marker
- Scissors
- Jewelry hardware or safety pin
- White glue
- Wax paper

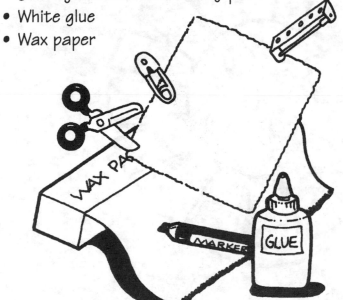

1. Draw a small colorful design on a piece of watercolor paper.
2. With a black permanent marker, outline the design and add details.
3. Cut out your design and place it on a piece of wax paper.
4. Apply a heavy coat of white glue to the cutout. Let it dry thoroughly.
5. Glue a safety pin or jewelry pin hardware to the back of the cutout.

Step 2

Step 5

MORE IDEAS

- Make two cutouts, following the directions above. Use a needle to poke a hole through the top of each piece. Attach jewelry hardware to make earrings for pierced ears.
- Make many cutouts. Poke holes through their centers and thread them into a necklace or bracelet.
- Make jewelry by alternating cutouts with bread clay beads (see page 87).

Paper Plate Sunflower

A Vase of Sunflowers Will Brighten Your Day

Paper Plate Sunflower

- Paper plate
- 2 yards (1.8 cm) of 1 ½" (3.75 cm) yellow ribbon, cut into 5" (12.5 cm) lengths
- Paint stirrer stick or old wooden ruler
- Sunflower seeds or brown buttons
- Glue
- Cardboard or poster board
- Brown and green tempera paint
- Paintbrush

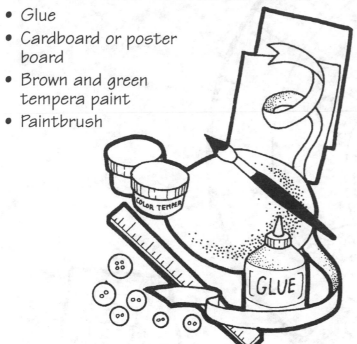

1. Cut a 5" (12.5 cm) circle from the center of a paper plate. Paint the circle brown and let it dry.
2. Glue the ends of the ribbon strips to form loops. Let the loops dry and then glue them around the edge of the blossom.
3. Glue buttons or sunflower seeds to the center of the blossom.
4. Glue the flower to the top of the ruler.
5. Cut two leaf shapes from the cardboard and glue them to the ruler (stem). Paint the leaves and the stem green.

Step 3

Step 5

MORE IDEAS

- Use strips of yellow construction paper or manila envelope for the flower petals.
- Make several sunflowers and plant them in a decorated clay pot filled with florist's foam or crumpled newspaper.
- Use sunflower heads only to decorate packages.

Ship's Porthole

Gaze Out on the Wonders of the Deep

Ship's Porthole

- Two paper plates
- Scissors
- Glue
- Stapler
- Crayons or markers
- Plastic wrap
- Sand or cornmeal
- Pebbles
- Yarn, sponge, tissue, or fabric
- Goldfish-shaped crackers

1. Color the center of one paper plate to look like water.

2. Glue sand and pebbles to the bottom of the water.

3. Using pieces of yarn, sponge, tissue, and fabric, create sea plants and animals and glue them to the water. Glue on some cracker goldfish.

4. Cut out the center section of the second plate, leaving the rim intact. Glue plastic wrap across the cutout opening to form the porthole's glass.

5. Staple the two plates together, rim to rim, with the water scene inside.

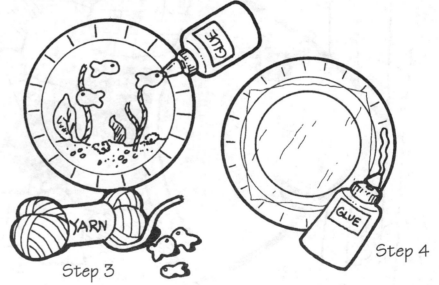

Step 3

Step 4

MORE IDEAS

- Create an outer space scene and the porthole of a space ship.
- Use colored plastic wrap or cellophane as the porthole glass.
- Create a fantasy scene and a dream porthole.

Stained Glass Fish

Hang This Colorful Fish in a Sunny Window

Stained Glass Fish

MATERIALS

- Wax paper, 9" x 12" (23 cm x 30 cm)
- Liquid starch
- Paintbrush
- Black crayon
- Tissue paper squares, 2"–3" (5 cm–8 cm)
- Construction paper
- Scissors
- Glue

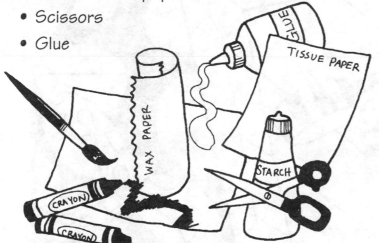

LET'S DO IT!!

1. With the black crayon, draw a large fish shape on the wax paper.
2. Cut out the fish shape, and paint it with liquid starch.
3. Cover the fish with tissue paper "scales," overlapping as desired, adding starch as needed for the pieces to stick. Let it dry.
4. Glue on construction paper details such as eyes, mouth, and fins.
5. Hang or tape the fish on a sunny window.

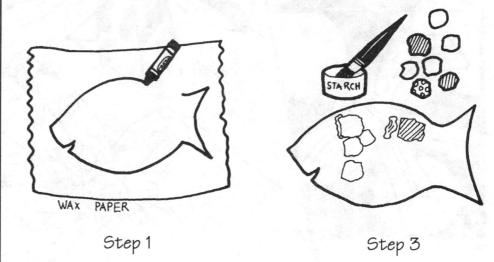

Step 1   Step 3

MORE IDEAS

- Make different stained glass objects such as flowers, hearts, or stars.
- Read **Rainbow Fish** by Marcus Pfister (North South, 1992).
- Make several smaller fish and create a mobile. Hang the fish from a wire hanger with fishing line. Hang strips of blue crepe paper for "water."

Paper Bow

Make Lots of Bows to Use for Decorations

Paper Bow

- Construction paper
- Glue
- Scissors

1. Cut a strip of construction paper and glue the ends together to form a circle.
2. Pinch the circle together in the center to form a bow and glue it together. Wrap and glue a smaller strip around the center of the bow.
3. Cut two strips of construction paper as wide as the bow and cut an inverted V in one end of each strip to form a ribbon.
4. Glue the straight ends of the ribbon to the back of the bow.
5. Glue the bow on a package for a decoration.

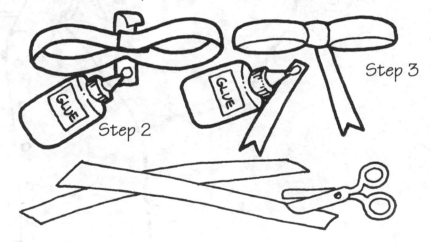

Step 3

Step 2

MORE IDEAS

- Make three construction paper circles as above and glue their centers together so the bows are at different angles.
- Make a curly bow. Wrap ½" (1.3 cm) strips of paper around a pencil and spray them with hair spray to form a curl. Pull the curls off of the pencil. Glue the curls on top of each other at different angles and use for decorations.
- Decorate the construction paper strips with crayon or markers before creating the bow and ribbons.

Paper Plate Pal

Make a New Friend Today

Paper Plate Pal

- Two paper plates
- Wire hanger
- Long-sleeved shirt
- Stapler
- Scissors
- Crayons or markers
- Yarn
- Construction paper

1. Draw a face on the bottom of a paper plate. Glue yarn hair to the plate.
2. Place the face plate over the hook portion of a hanger. Place the other paper plate face up under the hook. Staple the rims of the plates together.
3. Hang the shirt on the hanger and button it up.
4. Stuff the shirt sleeves and body with crumpled newspaper. Staple the shirttail front to the back.
5. Make hands from the construction paper and staple them to the shirt cuffs, also stapling the cuffs together.

Step 2   Step 5

MORE IDEAS

- Use buttons for eyes and yarn for eyebrows.
- Make a twin. Cut the face out of an 8" x 10" photograph of yourself and glue it to the bottom of a paper plate. Then, complete the directions as listed above.
- Make a complete person by attaching pants filled with crumpled newspaper. Sit your friend in a chair.

Lunch Bag Buddy

Make a Character From Lunch Bags

Lunch Bag Buddy

MATERIALS

- Three lunch sacks
- Newspaper, torn into strips
- String or yarn
- Crayons or markers
- Scissors
- Glue
- Tape
- Construction paper

1. Lay one sack flat with the opening at the bottom and draw the body of a character on it.

2. Stuff a second sack with newspaper strips and slide the body sack over the stuffed sack. Glue the sacks together and tie a string around the middle (waist).

3. Lay the third sack flat with the opening at the bottom and draw a face on it. Leave 3" (7.5 cm) under the chin. Stuff the sack with newspaper strips and tie the neck with string.

4. Glue or tape the head to the body. Add yarn hair and construction paper hands and feet.

GLUE

Step 2   Step 3

MORE IDEAS

- Use large grocery sacks to create a teddy bear.
- Make a character to fit the season, such as Santa Claus or a leprechaun.
- Make a sack family, using different sized bags for the family members.

Newspaper Fan

MATERIALS

- Newspaper, cut into rectangle
- Scissors
- Yarn or ribbon
- Hole punch
- Watercolor paints
- Paintbrush
- Stapler or tape

LET'S DO IT!!

1. Watercolor paint both sides of the newspaper, making several bands of color. Let it dry thoroughly.
2. Accordion pleat the sheet of newspaper and tape or staple one end.
3. Make a bow out of yarn or ribbon and attach it to the fastened end.
4. Punch holes along the top edge of the fan and weave ribbon through the holes. Tape or staple the end pieces to the fan.

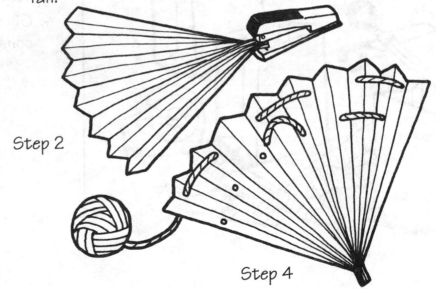

Step 2

Step 4

MORE IDEAS

- Weave more than one row of ribbon or yarn through the top of the fan.
- Before folding the newspaper into accordion pleats, decorate both sides with glitter or sequins.
- Make several fans and arrange them as a wall hanging in your bedroom.

Kitchen Capers

Pretzel Log Cabin

Construct a Pioneer Log Cabin

Pretzel Log Cabin

- ½ pint (250 mL) milk carton, cleaned and dried
- Stick pretzels
- Glue
- Wax paper
- Table knife
- Construction paper

1. Cover your work surface with wax paper.
2. Make windows and a door from construction paper and glue them in place onto the carton.
3. With a table knife, cut pretzels to fit the sides and the top of the milk carton and around the door and windows.
4. Glue one pretzel at a time onto the sides and the top of the carton until it is covered.

Step 2   Step 4

MORE IDEAS

- Using a brown crayon, draw the outline of a log cabin on drawing paper. Then fill in the outline with pretzel logs.
- Create a log fort. Use four quart-sized (0.95 L) milk cartons for towers. Attach stockade walls made of poster board or cardboard. Cover the entire structure with pretzels.
- Poke a hole through the top of the carton, tie on a string hanger, and use the log cabin as a Christmas ornament.

Sugar Cube Igloo

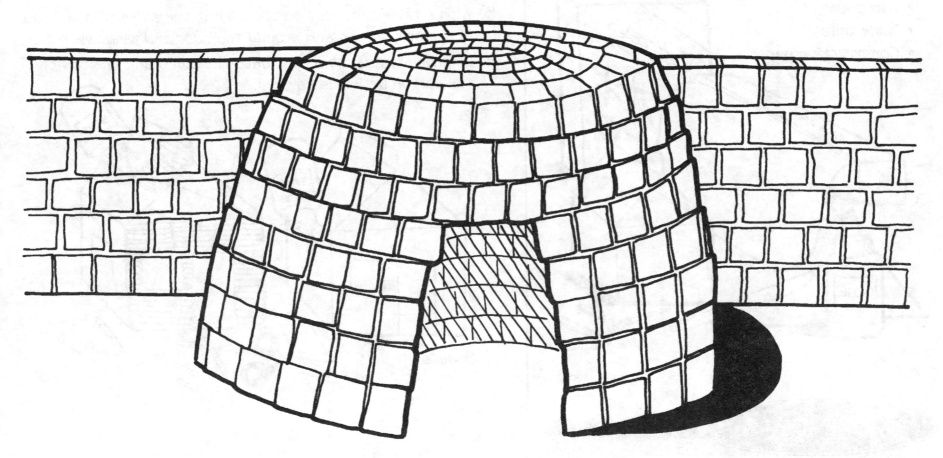

Build Your Own Home Sweet Home

Sugar Cube Igloo

- Sugar cubes
- Glue
- Cardboard, 12" x 12" (30 cm x 30 cm)
- Wax paper
- Black crayon
- Confectioners' sugar

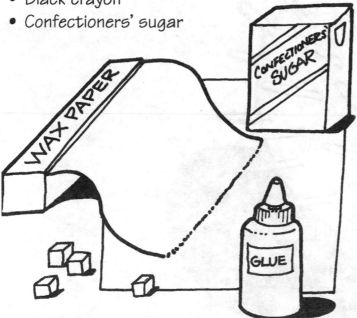

1. Cover the cardboard with wax paper. Using a black crayon, draw a 6" (15.25 cm) circle on the wax paper.

2. Lay a row of sugar cubes round the circle, leaving space for a door. Apply a line of glue to the cubes and lay another row of cubes on top, using one or two fewer cubes.

3. Continue this pattern for eight or nine rows, creating the top of the doorway by the sixth row.

4. Create a circular roof by gluing several cubes together in a circle. When this piece is dry, glue it to the top of the igloo as the roof.

5. Sprinkle the igloo and surrounding ground with confectioners' sugar to simulate snow.

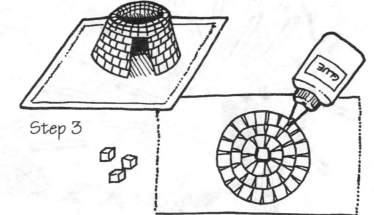

Step 3

Step 4

MORE IDEAS

- Glue an archway of cubes around the doorway to the igloo.
- Build sugar cube walls around the igloo.
- Cover the sides of a half-pint (250 mL) milk carton with sugar cubes. Use graham cracker halves for the roof.

Potato Hedgehog

This Little Animal Has a Prickly Personality

Potato Hedgehog

- Potato
- Toothpicks
- Uncooked spaghetti, broken into 1" (2.5 cm) pieces
- Felt
- Glue
- Small rubber bands

1. Break eight toothpicks in half. Using rubber bands, bundle the pieces in groups of four with the points at one end.
2. Stick the pointed ends of the toothpick bundles into the potato to create legs.
3. Glue on felt facial features.
4. Poke holes into the hedgehog with a toothpick.
5. Stick spaghetti pieces into the holes until the hedgehog is covered with prickles.

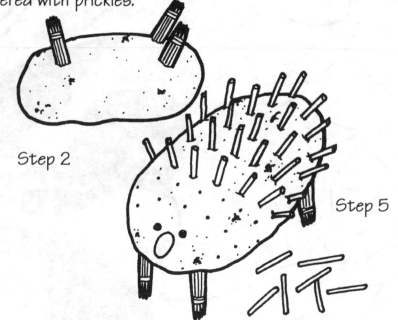

Step 2

Step 5

MORE IDEAS

- Read **The Tale of Mrs. Tiggywinkle** by Beatrix Potter (Dover, 1905) which features a hedgehog.
- Use a Styrofoam egg shape and toothpicks for a more permanent hedgehog.
- Listen to "Peer Gynt Suite" by Edvard Grieg. Does this music sound as if it's from a cartoon about a hedgehog?

Pasta Butterfly

This Pretty Butterfly Will Remind You of Spring All Year Round

Pasta Butterfly

- Toothpick
- Bow tie pasta
- Acrylic paint
- Glue
- Black permanent marker
- Wooden bead

1. Break the toothpick in half. Glue the toothpick antennae to the center of a piece of bow tie pasta.
2. Glue the bead head on top of the antennae.
3. Paint the butterfly.
4. Using the black marker, draw a face on the head.

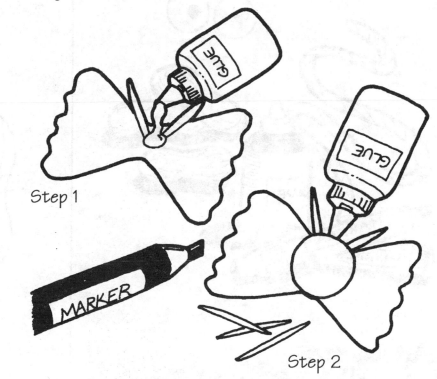

Step 1

Step 2

MORE IDEAS

- Use pipe cleaners for antennae.
- Decorate the butterfly wings with glitter or sequins.
- Glue a safety pin or jewelry pin to the back of the butterfly and wear it on your shirt.

Peanut Puppets

- Peanuts in the shell
- Wiggly eyes
- Glue
- Yarn
- Marker

1. Break off the bottom of a peanut shell and remove the peanut(s).
2. Enlarge the hole in the peanut until you are able to insert a finger.
3. Draw a face on the top part of the shell.
4. Glue on wiggly eyes and yarn hair.

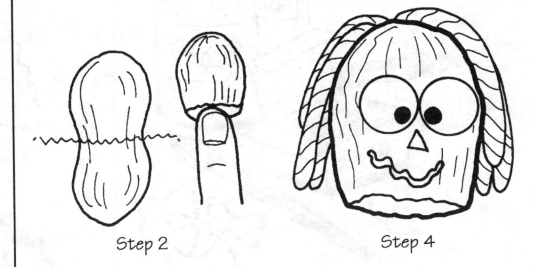

Step 2

Step 4

MORE IDEAS

- Create standing peanut animals. Stick four lengths of pipe cleaner into a peanut for legs. Bend the pipe cleaners to create feet. Draw on features.
- Make alien creatures, using pipe cleaners for antennae.
- Make peanut characters to fit on the ends of pencils instead of your finger. Give the pencils with peanut characters as party favors.

Candy-Cup Magnet

- Small candy-cup or cupcake liner
- Glue
- Jelly beans
- Small magnet

1. Glue the magnet to the back of the cupcake liner, pressing them together until the glue is dry.
2. Glue jelly beans into the cupcake liner. Make sure that the jelly beans are also glued together.
3. Allow them to dry thoroughly.
4. Glue small magnet to the bottom of the cup.
5. Paint the cup and jelly beans (but not the magnet) with thinned white glue to give it a shiny finish.

Step 1   Step 2

MORE IDEAS

- Coat the cup and candy with varnish or clear fingernail polish.
- Use different fillers such as candy hearts, cinnamon red-hots, or candy-coated chocolates.
- Use the candy-cup magnets to hold messages on your refrigerator.

Jelly Bean Strawberry

Double Your Fun With Candy Fruit

48

Jelly Bean Strawberry

- Plastic sandwich bag
- Red jelly beans
- Black permanent marker
- Rubber band
- Green construction paper
- Hole punch
- Scissors
- Glue

1. Put 15 jelly beans into one corner of a sandwich bag. Tie off the corner with a rubber band.
2. Cut off the excess plastic bag above the rubber band.
3. Cut strawberry cap leaves out of green construction paper and punch a hole in the middle.
4. Push the leaves onto the top of the strawberry and glue them into place.
5. Using a black marker, draw seeds on the outside of the strawberry.

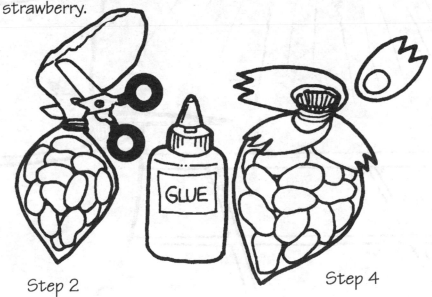

Step 2

Step 4

MORE IDEAS

- Use a square of plastic wrap instead of a sandwich bag and more jelly beans to create a larger, rounder fruit.
- Make oranges using orange jelly beans and glue on construction paper leaves.
- To create a carrot, make a cone from clear cellophane and tape it closed. Fill the cone with orange jelly beans and twist it closed. Glue Easter grass to the carrot top.

Hairy Potato Head

Watch This Potato Head Grow Wild Green Hair

Hairy Potato Head

- Potato
- Cotton balls
- Radish seeds
- Construction paper
- Pins or glue
- Scissors
- Knife
- Toothpicks
- Cup

1. Slice the top off a potato and carve out a hole in the potato large enough for the cotton balls.
2. Create facial features out of construction paper and glue or pin them in place on the potato.
3. Fill the hole with cotton balls, moisten them, and sprinkle them with the radish seeds.
4. Poke three toothpicks into different sides of the potato and place it in a cup on a windowsill.
5. Keep the cotton moist so the seed hair sprouts and grows.

Step 3

Step 4

MORE IDEAS

- Use other quick-sprouting seeds such as watercress, rye grass, alfalfa, or marigold.
- Make hairy eggheads by emptying an eggshell and following the procedures above.
- Make a sweet-potato head. Decorate the face as above but don't plant hair. Stick toothpicks around the sides to support the potato in a cup. Keep the cup filled with water and let the sweet potato sprout its own hair.

Candy Monster

Grocery List

Eggs
bread

wrap

butter

Juice

Make a Monster With Leftover Candy

52

Candy Monster

- Foam meat tray
- Large gumball
- Cinnamon red-hots
- Stick gum
- Shoestring licorice
- Black licorice bits
- Scissors
- Toothpick
- Knife

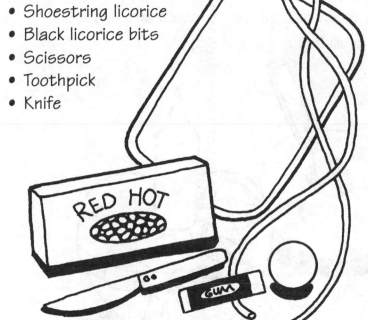

1. Cut a large circle from the foam meat tray.
2. Cut a large gumball in half. Glue a cinnamon red-hot in the center of each gumball half to make eyes. Glue the eyes onto the foam circle.
3. Glue on a red-hot for a nose and triangles cut from sticks of gum for teeth.
4. For licorice hair poke holes in the foam with a toothpick and then put glue on the ends of the licorice and insert it into the holes.

Step 2   Step 3

MORE IDEAS

- Glue a magnet to the back of your monster and use it on the refrigerator to hold messages.
- Create a silly face or happy face instead of a monster face. Use different candies such as jelly beans, gumdrops, or chocolate-covered candies.
- Make curly hair by cutting thin strips of stick gum and wrapping them around a pencil.

Apple Votive Candle

- Apple
- White candle
- Fresh leaves
- Ribbon
- Apple corer or knife
- Straight pins

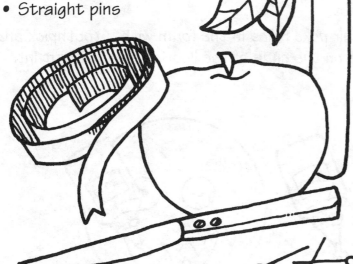

1. Choose an apple that stands fairly straight.
2. Core the apple from the top, being careful not to pierce the bottom.
3. Insert the candle into the hole in the apple.
4. Pin leaves into the apple at the base of the candle.
5. Tie a bow of ribbon around the apple.

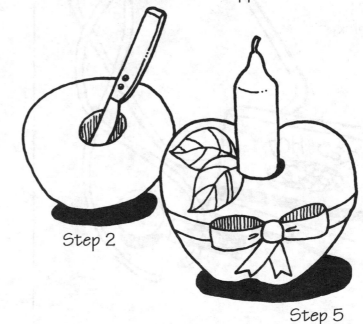

Step 2

Step 5

MORE IDEAS

- If the apple tends to roll, use a small ball of play clay to hold it steady.
- Glue bay leaves or cinnamon sticks around a short, fat candle; tie a ribbon bow around the candle.
- Make a fragrant orange votive candle. Using a toothpick, pierce a design around the orange and stick whole cloves into the holes. Cut an X into the top of the orange and push in a candle. Use a small ball of play clay to keep the orange from rolling.

Gumdrop Construction

MATERIALS

LET'S DO IT!!

- Toothpicks

- Gumdrops

1. Poke toothpicks into gumdrops.

2. Attach gumdrops to the other ends of the toothpicks.

3. Stick toothpicks into the gumdrops at different angles to form walls.

4. Build a house.

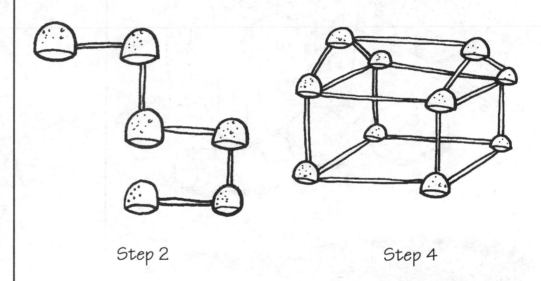

Step 2   Step 4

MORE IDEAS

- Construct a bridge, pyramid, or other structure.
- Build structures using toothpicks and mini marshmallows or straws and large marshmallows.
- Tape construction paper to toothpicks to create walls and roofs.

Candy Necklace

- Dental floss
- Blunt-tip tapestry needle
- Assorted candies and gumballs (Candies need not have holes if they are soft enough to be pierced with a needle, but they should not easily melt.)

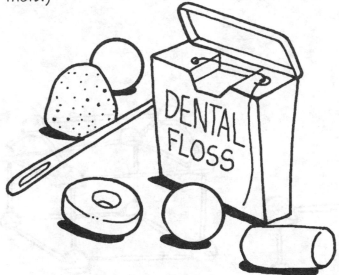

1. Thread the tapestry needle with 30" (76 cm) of dental floss and knot the ends together.
2. String the first piece of candy onto the floss and tie the floss around the candy to act as a large knot. Leave a long dental floss tail.
3. String more candies and gumballs until the dental floss is nearly covered. Leave a tail.
4. Cut the needle off the floss and tie the dental floss tails together to form a necklace.

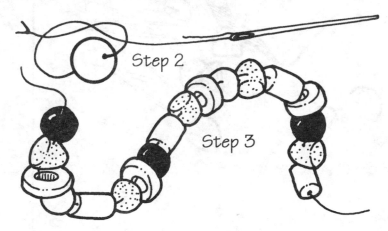

Step 2

Step 3

MORE IDEAS

- Use a thimble to help you push the needle through the candy. Or ask a parent to help you by poking holes through the goodies with an ice pick.
- A necklace of gumballs only is very pretty and will last for quite some time if the gumballs remain dry.
- Licorice twists can be cut and used as long beads—string them the long way or pierce them and let them hang as pendants.
- Younger children can string candies and cereals with holes onto shoestring licorice.

Dyed Rice Mosaic

MATERIALS

- 4 cups (about 1,000 mL) uncooked rice
- Food coloring—4 colors
- 4 plastic resealable bags
- 4 sheets wax paper
- 4 bowls
- Poster board or cardboard
- Crayons
- Glue

LET'S DO IT!!

1. Put one cup of rice in each plastic bag. Place five drops of different food coloring into each of the bags, seal them, and shake them until the rice is coated.

2. Pour each color of rice onto a piece of wax paper and allow it to dry.

3. Place the dried and dyed rice into separate bowls.

4. Using crayons, draw a background scene on poster board.

5. Glue the colored rice onto the picture and let it dry.

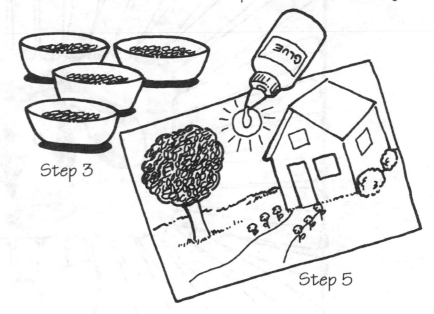

Step 3

Step 5

MORE IDEAS

- Dye and use popped popcorn as described above.
- Dye and use bits of eggshell. (See the Safety Guidelines on page 7.) Use five drops of food coloring and one tablespoon (15 mL) of vinegar to dye the eggshells.
- Dye and use different-shaped pasta for mosaics.

Cinnamon Stick Frame

Put Your Favorite Photo in a Fragrant Frame

Cinnamon Stick Frame

- Two 4" x 6" (10 cm x 15.25 cm) pieces of poster board
- Pencil
- Scissors
- Glue
- Cinnamon sticks
- Ribbon
- Paper clip

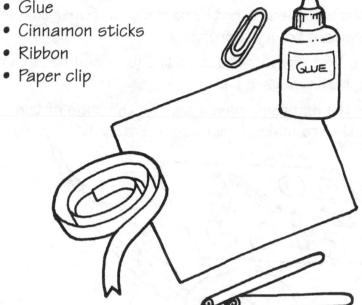

1. Cut out a 3" x 5" (7 cm x 13 cm) center from one piece of poster board, leaving a frame.
2. Glue cinnamon sticks around the edge of the frame and add a ribbon bow.
3. Glue the sides and bottom of the frame to the second piece of poster board.
4. Slip a photograph in the top of the frame so it is visible through the cutout center.
5. Glue a paper clip to the back of the frame to use as a hanger.

Step 2

Step 5

MORE IDEAS

- Cover the frame with materials gathered from nature, such as acorns, seeds, seed pods, or shells.
- Glue old puzzle pieces onto the frame. When the glue has dried, paint the frame all one color or paint the puzzle pieces in different colors.
- Make a frame from craft sticks. Glue the ends of four craft sticks together and decorate with paint, glitter, or sequins. Glue or tape a photo behind the frame.

Pretty Pasta Jewelry

- Variety of pasta with holes through the centers
- Yarn or string
- Scissors
- Food coloring
- 4 bowls
- Rubbing alcohol
- Paper towels

1. To dye the pasta, fill each bowl half full of rubbing alcohol. Add several drops of food coloring and the pasta.

2. Let the pasta remain in the mixture until the pieces are the color you want.

3. Pour off the liquid and turn the pasta onto paper towels. Allow the pieces to dry thoroughly.

4. String the first pasta piece onto the yarn and tie a knot around it, leaving a yarn tail.

5. String on the remaining pasta and tie the ends of the yarn together to make a necklace or bracelet.

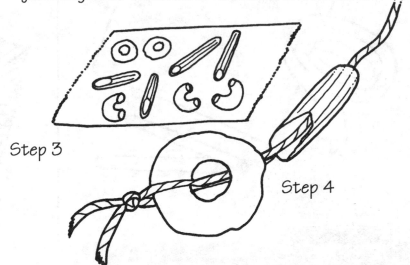

Step 3

Step 4

MORE IDEAS

- Wrap one end of the yarn with tape to create a needle.
- Alternate pasta pieces with clay beads (page 87).
- Using acrylic paints, decorate the pasta pieces with funny and wild designs.

Natural Necessities

Nuthead Magnet

This Perky Face Happily Holds Your Refrigerator Messages

62

Nuthead Magnet

- Whole nut in the shell
- Acrylic paints
- Fine-tipped paintbrush
- Yarn
- Small flat magnet
- Glue

1. Paint a face on a nut and let it dry thoroughly.
2. Cut out and glue on yarn hair.
3. Glue a small magnet to the back of the nuthead.

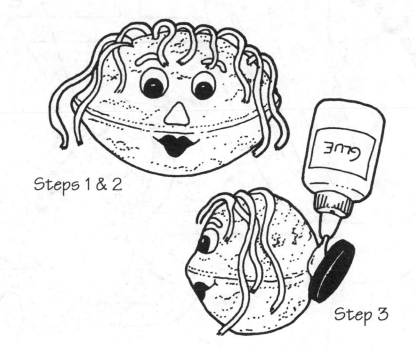

Steps 1 & 2

Step 3

MORE IDEAS

- Bend a paper clip into the shape of eyeglasses; glue them to the nuthead.
- Glue the nut to the end of a craft stick to make a nuthead puppet. Add fabric clothing.

Leaf Person Suncatcher

Hang This Happy Person to Catch the Sun in Your Window

Leaf Person Suncatcher

- Broad, flat leaf
- Assorted flowers, petals, pieces of bark, feathers
- Glue
- Clear contact paper
- Hole punch
- Ribbon or string

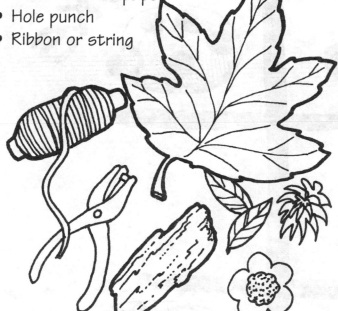

1. Lay a piece of contact paper sticky side up and place the leaf on it.
2. Glue the collected materials on the leaf to create facial features. (If the items are too thick or too moist, the contact paper will not stick.)
3. Carefully place another piece of contact paper over the top of the leaf face and press both pieces together.
4. Trim around the face, leaving a ½" (1.3 cm) border.
5. Punch a hole in the top and tie a loop of ribbon through it to use as a hanger.

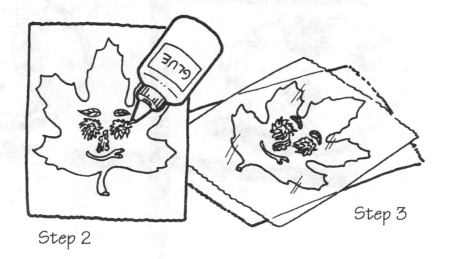

Step 2

Step 3

MORE IDEAS

- Use bits of feathers for hair, eyebrows, mustache, or other features.
- Use flowers for eyes (flat flowers work best).
- Using a warm iron, press leaves between two sheets of wax paper.

Animal Tic-Tac-Toe Rocks

These Pets Are Always Ready to Play

MATERIALS

- 10 smooth rocks, about 1 ½" (3.75 cm) in diameter
- Acrylic paints
- Paintbrush
- Chalk

LET'S DO IT!!

1. Paint five rocks red. Paint on black details to make the rocks look like ladybugs.

2. Paint the other five rocks yellow. Paint on black details to make the rocks look like butterflies.

3. Make a tic-tac-toe game board on the sidewalk, using chalk.

4. Find a partner and enjoy your game!

Step 1   Step 2

MORE IDEAS

- Create game pieces that look like other animals such as bees and birds or cats and dogs.
- Make a permanent game board by painting a tic-tac-toe grid on a piece of cardboard.
- Make a pet rock. Use a large rock for the body, four pebbles for feet, and a small rock for the head. Glue them together, paint your pet, and give it a name.

Leaf Covered Box

Use This as a Gift Box or to Hold Your Treasures

Leaf Covered Box

- Shoe box with lid
- Tempera paint
- Assortment of leaves
- Wax paper
- Stacks of books
- Glue
- Water
- Paintbrush

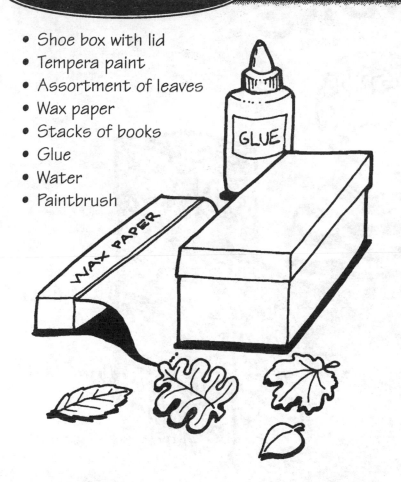

1. Place the leaves between two pieces of wax paper and press them under a stack of books for several days to flatten them.
2. Paint the shoe box and the lid and let them dry thoroughly.
3. In a bowl, mix water and glue to the consistency of paint.
4. Place a leaf on the box and brush on glue to attach the leaf.
5. Continue adding leaves until the box and lid are covered.

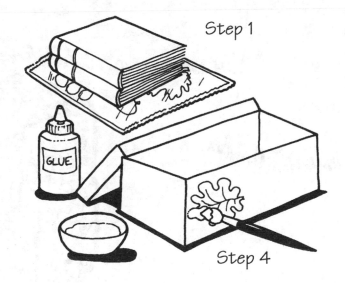

Step 1

Step 4

MORE IDEAS

- Make paper bows to decorate the box (see page 30).
- Paint the leaves.
- Spatter-paint the box, using a toothbrush (see page 17).

Mud Bricks

Like Getting Dirty? This Is for You!

Mud Bricks

- ½ pint (250 mL) cartons
- Dirt and sand
- Grass clippings, leaves, and twigs
- Water
- Dish tub

1. Cut the cartons in half to form brick molds.
2. Put dirt, sand, clippings, leaves, and twigs into a dish tub.
3. Add water to make a thick mud mixture and stir it (with your hands, of course!).
4. Pour the mud into the molds, place them in the sunshine, and allow them to harden.
5. Peel the cartons off the bricks and build away!

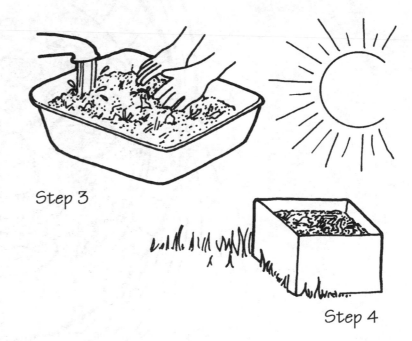

Step 3

Step 4

MORE IDEAS

- Use pie or cake tins to make mud pies and cakes. Decorate them with twigs and leaves.
- Use your mud bricks to build a fort.
- Read **Muddigush** (Macmillan, 1992) by Kimberly Knutson.

Nature Mask

Make a Mask Using Gatherings From Nature

Nature Mask

- Paper plate
- Stapler
- Scissors
- Large rubber band
- Items collected from nature, such as leaves, pods, and feathers
- Glue

1. Cut mouth, eye, and nose holes in the paper plate.
2. Staple the rubber band to the sides of the plate.
3. On the front of the plate, glue the items you found in nature.

Step 3

MORE IDEAS

- Make your mask look like a specific animal. Use construction paper to help you make its features.
- Make a nature headband. Cut a construction paper strip to fit around your head. Glue on leaves and feathers and let the glue dry. Then, staple the ends together to form a headband.
- Using the same process as for the headband, make a nature bracelet and choker necklace. Wrap the paper bands around your neck or wrist and staple the ends together.

Dandelion Jewelry

MATERIALS

- Dandelion flowers
- Dental floss
- Blunt-tip tapestry needle
- Scissors

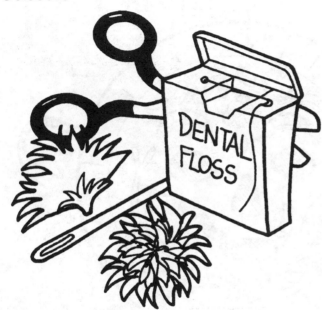

LET'S DO IT!!

1. Thread the needle with dental floss. Double the floss, make sure it fits around your neck or wrist and knot the ends together, leaving a dental floss tail.
2. String dandelion heads onto the floss until the floss is nearly covered.
3. Cut the needle off the floss and tie the dental floss tails together to form a necklace.

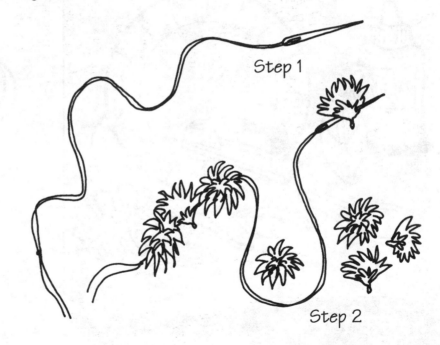

Step 1

Step 2

MORE IDEAS

- Pin a dandelion flower head on your shirt.
- Alternate dandelion flower heads with leaves or other kinds of flowers. (Get permission to pick them!)
- Read **Amy Loves the Sun** (Harper, 1988) by Julia Hoban.

Clay Dough Creations

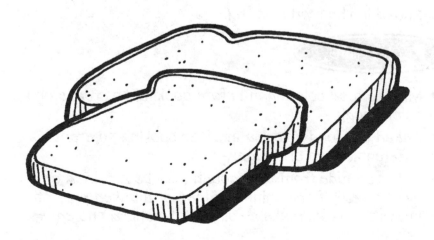

Clay Recipes

Flour Clay

- 2 cups (500 mL) flour
- 1 cup (250 mL) water
- 1 cup (250 mL) salt
- 2 tablespoons (30 mL) alum
- 2 tablespoons (30 mL) salad oil
- Food coloring
- Bowl

LET'S DO IT!!

1. Knead all the ingredients together in a bowl until the mixture is smooth and pliable.
2. Knead in the food coloring.

RECIPE TIPS

- Wear rubber gloves when kneading in the food coloring to prevent staining your hands.
- Separate the dough into balls and knead in different colors of food coloring to make different colored clay.

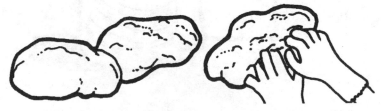

Cornstarch Clay

MATERIALS

- 1 cup (250 mL) cornstarch
- 2 cups (500 mL) baking soda
- 1 ½ cups (375 mL) cold water
- Food coloring
- Saucepan and spoon
- Wax paper

LET'S DO IT!!

1. Mix all the ingredients together in a saucepan.
2. Cook over a low heat, stirring constantly until the mixture clumps together.
3. Turn the mixture out onto wax paper.
4. Knead the dough until it is smooth and pliable.
5. Knead in the food coloring.

RECIPE TIPS

- Mix the food coloring in before cooking to create one-color dough.
- Knead the food coloring in after cooking to create different colors of dough.
- Objects made from this dough may be air dried or oven baked. If the thinner edges of a baked project brown too fast, make a foil tent to shield the edges.

Clay Recipes (cont.)

Bread Clay

MATERIALS

- 5 pieces of white bread with crusts trimmed off
- 5 teaspoons (25 mL) liquid dishwashing soap
- 5 tablespoons (75 mL) white glue
- Food coloring
- Bowl

LET'S DO IT!!

1. Tear the bread into bits and place it in a bowl.
2. Add the dishwashing soap and glue.
3. Knead together until the mixture no longer sticks to your hands.
4. Knead in the food coloring.

RECIPE TIPS

- Make sure your hands are clean before kneading, or the clay may turn a dirty gray color.
- Use wheat bread to make brown dough to use for naturally "antiqued" objects.
- Wear rubber gloves when kneading in the food coloring to prevent staining your hands.

Salt Clay

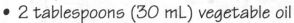

MATERIALS

- 2 cups (500 mL) flour
- ½ cup (125 mL) salt
- 2 tablespoons (30 mL) vegetable oil
- ½ cup–¾ cup (125 mL–180 ml) water
- Food coloring
- Bowl
- Cookie sheet

LET'S DO IT!!

1. Mix together the flour, salt, and oil in a bowl.
2. Add ½ cup (120 mL) of water and knead. Add more water as necessary to make the dough smooth and pliable.
3. Knead in the food coloring.
4. To bake objects made from the dough, place them on a cookie sheet. Bake them at 350° F (177° C) until they are golden brown and firm to a gentle touch.

RECIPE TIPS

- If the thinner edges of a baked project brown too fast, make a foil tent to shield the edges.
- Wear rubber gloves when kneading in the food coloring to prevent staining your hands.

Birthday Candle Holders

Use These with Curly Ribbon on Top of a Party Cake

Birthday Candle Holders

- Batch of cornstarch clay in several different colors
- Birthday candles
- Pasta letters
- Sequins
- Wax paper

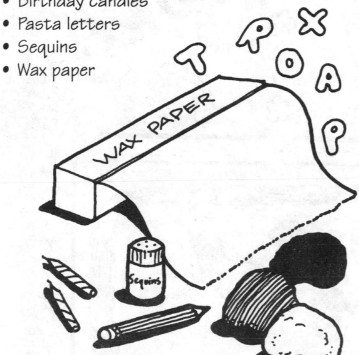

1. Form a small ball of clay, about 1 ½" (3.75 cm) across.
2. Place the ball onto a sheet of wax paper and press gently to flatten the bottom.
3. Push a birthday candle into the middle of the rounded, top part of the clay ball to create a hole.
4. Let the candle holder dry thoroughly.
5. Glue pasta letters, sequins, and small bits of colored clay onto the candle holder.

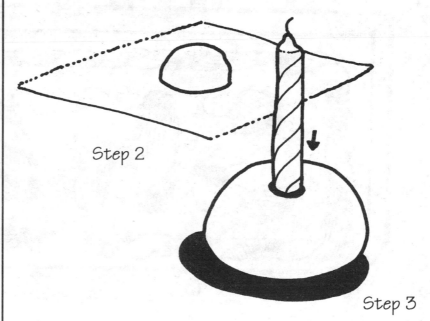

Step 2

Step 3

MORE IDEAS

- Put a small wax paper circle between the clay holder and the birthday cake.
- Make a larger holder for a larger candle.
- Form different clay shapes for the candle holders, such as stars, squares, or flowers.

Hanging Nameplate

Personalize Your Room with This Nameplate

Hanging Nameplate

- Cornstarch clay in several different colors
- Table knife
- Paper clip
- Rolling pin
- Small bowl of water
- Wax paper

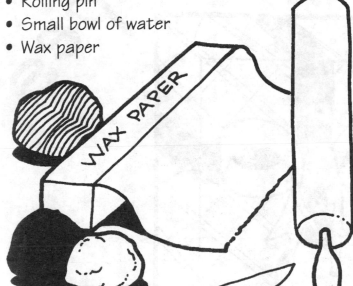

1. Form a ball of clay and place it on a sheet of wax paper.
2. With a rolling pin, roll the ball of clay into a slab about ½" (1.3 cm) thick.
3. Use a table knife to form the slab into a rectangle, circle, square, or star shape.
4. Twist different colors of clay to write a name and trim the nameplate. Use water to stick the twisted trim to the nameplate.
5. Push a paper clip halfway into the top edge of the nameplate to use as a hanger.

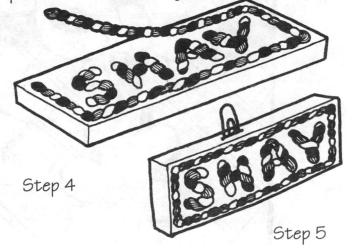

Step 4

Step 5

MORE IDEAS

- Make a multicolored or rainbow nameplate by blending several colors of clay together before rolling out the nameplate.
- Use the nameplate as a personalized paperweight.
- Make a flat oval clay lake. Make some clay waves on the lake and make a surfer or boat to put on the waves. Use this as a decoration or a paperweight.

Cinnamon Scented Shapes

Enjoy These Wonderfully Fragrant Shapes All Year Round

Cinnamon Scented Shapes

MATERIALS

- ½ cup (125 mL) cinnamon
- 1 tablespoon (15 mL) ground cloves
- ⅜ cup (90 mL) applesauce
- 3 tablespoons (75 mL) white glue
- Cookie cutters in assorted shapes
- Wire rack
- Toothpick
- Yarn

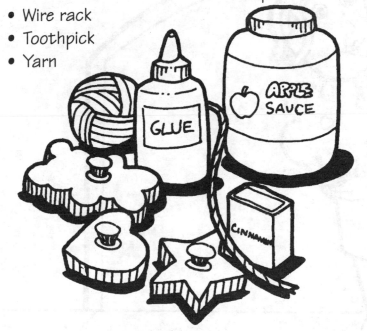

LET'S DO IT!!

1. Stir the cinnamon, applesauce, and glue together and knead until the mixture is smooth.

2. Pat the dough to about ¼" (0.63 cm) thick. Use cookie cutters to cut out shapes.

3. Poke a hole through the top of each shape with a toothpick and allow the shapes to air dry for several days on a wire rack.

4. Thread yarn through the hole to use for hanging anywhere you want to enjoy the scent of cinnamon.

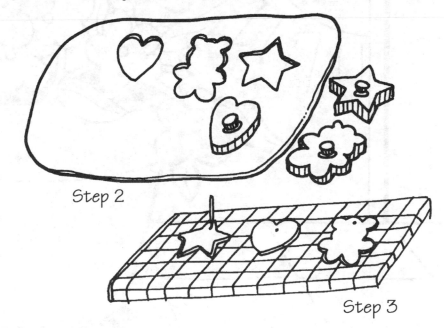

Step 2

Step 3

MORE IDEAS

- Poke holes through the sides of the shapes and tie the shapes together with yarn to make a swag.
- Use the shapes as package decorations or Christmas tree ornaments.
- Put a couple of these in your drawer to use as sachets.

Potted Plant Person

Poke This Person Into Your Favorite Potted Plant

Potted Plant Person

- Clay
- Plant support stick
- Garlic press
- Potted plant
- Acrylic paints
- Fine-tipped paintbrush

1. Form a head, nose, and ears from the clay.
2. Using a garlic press, create hair from the clay and attach the hair to the head, using a little water.
3. Push one end of the plant support stick into the bottom of the head. Push the other end into a potted plant.
4. Let the clay head dry thoroughly and then paint on the facial features.

Step 2

Step 3

MORE IDEAS

- Form the clay into different shapes such as animal heads, fruits, or vegetables.
- Make a magic wand by forming the clay into a star.
- Use the characters as stick puppets. Glue paper or fabric clothes onto the support stick.

Finger Puppets

MATERIALS

- Clay
- Wiggly eyes
- Elbow macaroni
- Glue
- Yarn
- Wax paper

LET'S DO IT!!

1. Mold clay around the tip of your finger.
2. Push in wiggly eyes and elbow macaroni for ears.
3. Remove the clay head carefully from your finger and put it on a sheet of wax paper until it is thoroughly dry.
4. Glue on yarn for hair. If the other features are loose, glue them on.

Step 2

Step 4

MORE IDEAS

- Use a garlic press to create clay hair.
- Make several puppets to stage a show.
- Paint your finger puppet with acrylic paints.

Bread Clay Beads

- Bread clay in various colors
- Bamboo skewer
- Several books
- Paints
- Paintbrush
- Spray varnish
- Yarn or ribbon

1. Form the clay into a variety of shapes such as balls, cubes, and short tubes.
2. Thread the beads onto a bamboo skewer, leaving 1" (2.5 cm) between each bead and let them dry thoroughly.
3. Paint the beads while they are still on the skewer.
4. Rest the ends of the skewer on two stacks of books to allow the paint to dry on all sides of the beads. When the paint dries, spray the beads with varnish.
5. String the dry beads onto yarn or ribbon to make necklaces or bracelets.

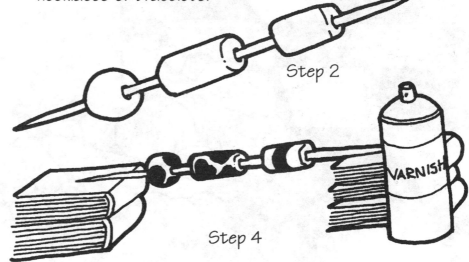

Step 2

Step 4

MORE IDEAS

- Use several different colors and string beads in a pattern.
- Make beads using two or three different colors on each bead. Make polka dots or swirls.
- Use beads instead of knots between hardware jewels. (See page 124.)

Clay Fruit Centerpiece

Tiny Fruits Make a Pretty Centerpiece

Clay Fruit Centerpiece

MATERIALS

- Double batch of bread clay
- Candle
- Acrylic paints
- Paintbrush
- Glue
- Spray varnish

LET'S DO IT!!

1. Shape some of the clay into a donut shape around a candle, remove the candle, and allow the clay ring to dry.
2. Shape the remaining clay into small fruit shapes such as pears, apples, oranges, or half-peeled bananas.
3. When the shapes are thoroughly dry, paint them.
4. Glue the fruit to the candle base.
5. When the glue is dry, spray the entire centerpiece with varnish.

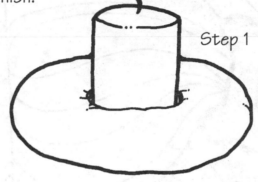

Step 1

Step 2

MORE IDEAS

- Poke holes in the clay fruit and string it for a necklace or bracelet.
- Make two of one kind of fruit, poke holes in the tops, and attach earring hardware.
- Make a cornucopia. Glue an ice cream cone on its side to a cardboard base. Paint the cone and base. Glue clay fruit spilling out from the cone. Spray the piece with varnish.

Bone Hair Clips

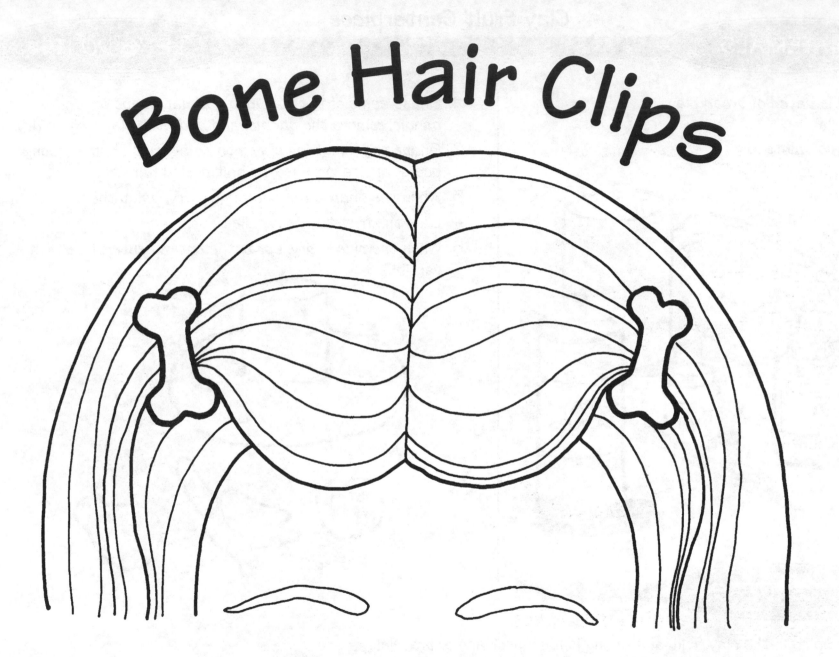

Make and Wear These Prehistoric Hair Ornaments

Bone Hair Clips

- One batch of bread clay made with wheat bread
- Spray varnish
- Glue
- Bobby pins

1. Shape the clay into bone shapes. Let the bones dry thoroughly.

2. Spray the bones with varnish and let them dry again.

3. Glue a bobby pin to the back of each bone.

4. Wear the bones in your hair, along with other prehistoric jewelry. (See pages 92 and 140.)

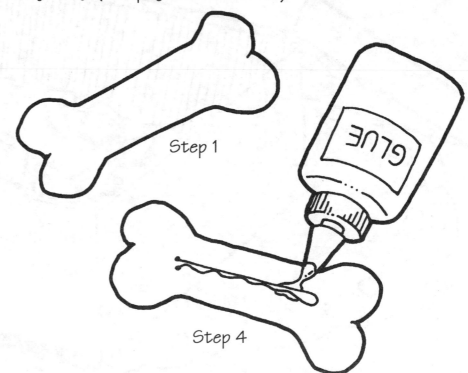

Step 1

Step 4

MORE IDEAS

- Punch holes in the clay bones before they dry and use as them as beads for a necklace.
- Make bone earrings by punching holes in them and attaching earring hardware.
- Glue clay bones around a photo frame and insert a picture of your dog.

Dinosaur Teeth Jewelry

Wear These for a Stone Age Effect

Dinosaur Teeth Jewelry

- One batch of salt clay
- Toothpick
- Cookie sheet
- Wire cooling rack
- Brown shoe polish
- Leather cord or brown yarn

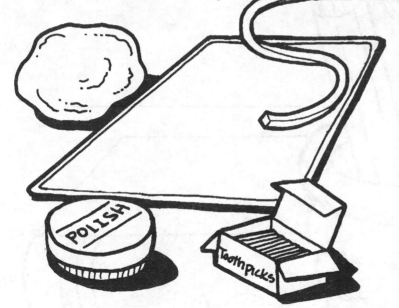

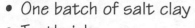

1. Imagine what dinosaur teeth looked like and shape the clay into many different tooth shapes.

2. With a toothpick, poke holes in the tops of the teeth.

3. Bake the teeth at 350° F (177° C) for 10 to 15 minutes on a lightly greased cookie sheet and let them cool on a wire rack.

4. Rub the teeth lightly with brown shoe polish to make them look old.

5. String the teeth onto cord or yarn to make a necklace and bracelet.

Step 1

Step 3

MORE IDEAS

- Alternate the dinosaur teeth with bones (page 90), pumice stones (page 140), and bread clay beads (page 87).
- Make clay bear claw jewelry.
- Draw and color a prehistoric scene with dinosaurs and other animals and glue clay teeth in their mouths.

Clay Coil Pot

Use This to Hold Pencils or Odds and Ends

Clay Coil Pot

- One batch of salt clay
- Cookie sheet
- Paints
- Paintbrush
- Spray varnish

1. Roll the clay into a long rope about ½" (1.3 cm) in diameter.

2. Coil the rope into a tight lollipop-type circle on a cookie sheet. This will be the pot's base.

3. Roll three or four more clay ropes. Around the edge of the base, coil the ropes up on top of each other to create a small pot. Use water to attach the coils together.

4. Bake the pot at 350° F (177° C) for 30 to 45 minutes. Let it cool thoroughly.

5. Paint the pot. When the paint is dry, coat the pot with spray varnish.

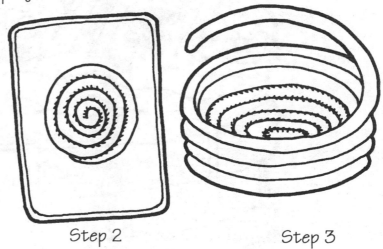

Step 2   Step 3

MORE IDEAS

- Make an arched opening in a pot and turn it upside down to look like a beehive.
- Coil a clay rope into a snake-shaped candle holder.
- Coil clay ropes tightly into lollipops, insert a craft stick in each, and paint them candy colors when they're dry. Do not cook the stick; it will burn. Use the lollipops as package decorations or party favors.

Woven Basket

Weave a Decorative Basket

Woven Basket

- One batch of salt clay
- Rolling pin
- Toothpicks
- Table knife
- Cookie sheet

LET'S DO IT!!

1. Roll out the clay to ¼" (0.63 cm) thickness. Cut out a 3" (7.5 cm) circle for the bottom of the basket. Cut the remaining dough into strips ½" (1.3 cm) wide.

2. Around the edge of the clay circle, insert toothpicks about ½" (1.3 cm) apart.

3. Gently weave the strips in and out of the toothpicks.

4. Create a rim and handle by making twisted clay ropes and attaching them to the top of the basket. Pinch the ends of the handle to the sides of the basket.

5. Bake the basket at 350° F (177° C) for about 30 to 45 minutes.

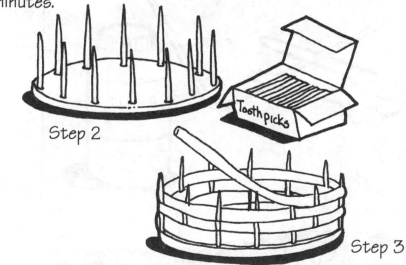

Step 2

Step 3

MORE IDEAS

- Try different sizes and shapes for the basket base.
- Paint the basket, let it dry, and spray it with varnish.
- Fill the basket with excelsior and goodies.

Bird's Nest

- One batch of salt clay
- Garlic press
- Cookie sheet
- Paints
- Paintbrush

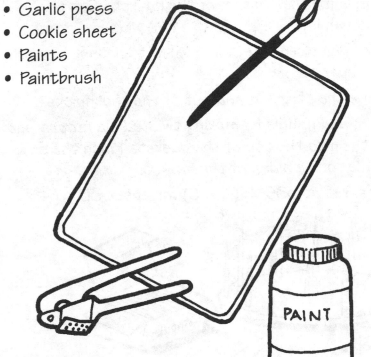

1. Run the clay through a garlic press, creating long, thin strips.
2. Form the strips into a nest.
3. Create a bird and eggs from the remaining clay.
4. Bake the nest at 350° F (177° C) until it is golden brown.
5. Paint the bird, nest, and eggs when they are cool.

Step 1

Step 3

MORE IDEAS

- Glue jelly beans or marbles in the nest for eggs.
- Insert a paper clip into the nest. Tie a loop of ribbon onto the paper clip and use the nest as a Christmas ornament.
- Use the nest as a paperweight.

Fabric Finery

Handkerchief Doll

Make a Huggable Doll—Without Sewing

Handkerchief Doll

- Handkerchief or 8" (20 cm) square of fabric
- Rubber band
- Cotton balls
- Fine tipped markers
- Lace

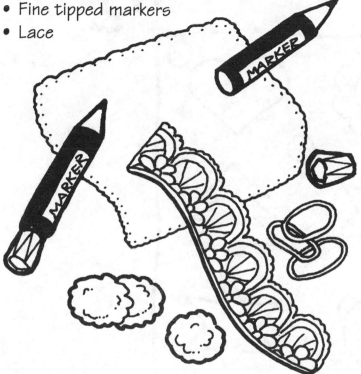

1. Place two or three cotton balls in the center of the handkerchief.
2. Pull the handkerchief up around the cotton balls and secure them inside with a rubber band, making a doll's head.
3. Tie an overhand knot in one tail of the handkerchief, close to the doll's head, to create an arm. Do the same with the opposite tail.
4. Draw a face on the doll.
5. Glue a ring of lace to frame the doll's face like a bonnet.

Step 2   Step 3

MORE IDEAS

- Draw a face with fabric crayons or glue on fabric facial features.
- Use print fabric and sew on buttons for facial features.
- Make a handkerchief doll family, using different sizes of fabric squares.

Quick No-Sew Quilt

It's Fun and Easy to Make This Charming Country Quilt

MATERIALS

- 12" (30 cm) square of white or light-colored fabric
- Paper-backed fusible webbing (available at fabric stores)
- 12 fabric squares, 3" x 3" (8 cm x 8 cm)
- Buttons
- Glue
- Pencil
- Scissors
- Iron

LET'S DO IT!!

1. Have an adult iron the fusible webbing to the small fabric squares, following the manufacturer's directions.

2. Draw shapes such as trees, pumpkins, apples, flowers, hearts, or bears on the paper back of the webbing, and cut out the shapes.

3. Remove the paper backing and arrange the cutouts in four rows and four columns on the large square of background fabric.

4. Have an adult iron the cutouts to the fabric square.

5. Glue on the buttons to decorate your quilt.

Step 3

Step 4

MORE IDEAS

- Turn your quilt square into a pillow by gluing three sides of your quilt front to another 12" (30 cm) square. Stuff the pouch with cotton and then glue the final edge together.
- Make two more squares and glue the edges together to make a wall hanging.
- Read **The Keeping Quilt** (Little Simon, 1988) by Patricia Polacco.

Gingham Cross-Stitch

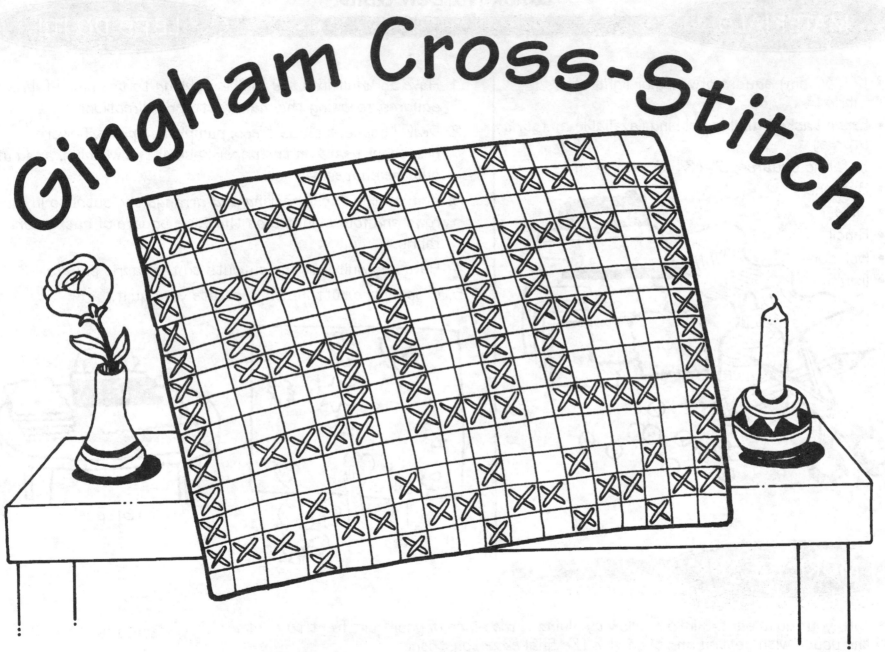

Stitch Your Name or a Design

Gingham Cross Stitch

- 8" (20 cm) square of gingham material
- Embroidery hoop
- Embroidery needle
- Embroidery thread
- Scissors

1. Secure the gingham in the embroidery hoop.
2. Thread the needle and knot the ends of the thread together.
3. Bring the needle up through the bottom of the fabric at the corner of one gingham square. Push the needle through the fabric in the diagonal corner to form half an X.
4. Repeat in the opposite corners of the same gingham square, completing the X.
5. Continue this process in gingham squares to form letters or a design.

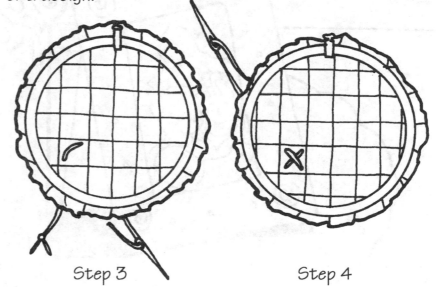

Step 3   Step 4

MORE IDEAS

- Use a variety of colored embroidery thread. Create a border around the large square.
- Use graph paper to plan your name or design before you stitch.
- Turn your cross-stitched square into a pillow (see page 103).

Keepsake Jar

Save Pennies or Other Small Treasurers in This Special Jar

Keepsake Jar

MATERIALS

- Canning jar with two-piece lid (outer ring and inner circle)
- Two 4" (10 cm) squares of white fabric
- Poster board circle, same size as inner circle of lid
- Lace
- Ribbon
- Glue
- Scissors
- Cotton balls

LET'S DO IT!!

1. Decorate the fabric squares with fabric paint or fabric crayons.

2. Layer the following face down in this order: (1) the jar lid ring, (2) one decorated fabric square, (3) the cotton balls, (4) the inner jar lid. Push the inner lid into place and trim off the excess fabric.

3. Cover the poster board circle with the other fabric square. Glue the excess fabric to the underside of the circle and then glue the circle to the inner jar lid with the decorated side face out.

4. Glue lace around the lower edge of the outer ring and tie a ribbon bow around the top edge of the lace. Screw the lid onto the jar.

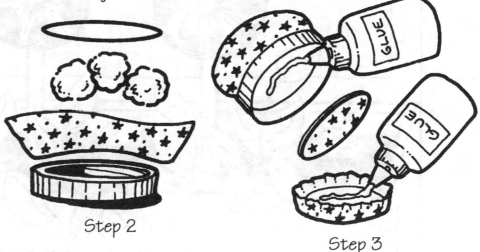

Step 2

Step 3

MORE IDEAS

- Fill the jar with jelly beans, chocolate kisses, or other candy and give it as a birthday present.
- Decorate the outside of the jar with acrylic paint.
- Fill the jar with sewing supplies, using the cotton-ball top as a pincushion.

Yo-Yo Flower

Create a Colorful Fabric Flower Garden

Yo-Yo Flower

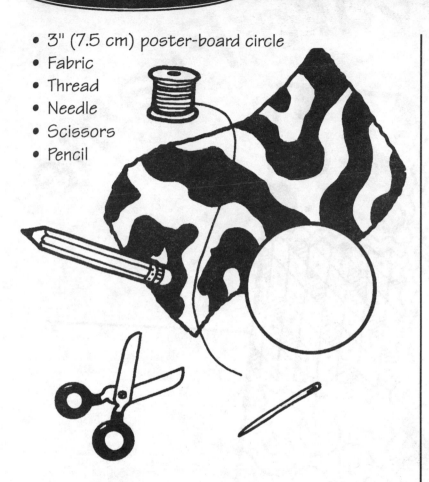

- 3" (7.5 cm) poster-board circle
- Fabric
- Thread
- Needle
- Scissors
- Pencil

1. Trace the circle on the underside of the fabric and cut out the fabric circle.
2. Thread the needle, knot the thread ends together, and stitch around the edge of the fabric circle.
3. Pull the thread tight to make a Yo-Yo shape.
4. To make a knot to secure the stitching, take a stitch but do not pull it tight. Run the needle under this stitch and then under it again and pull it tight.

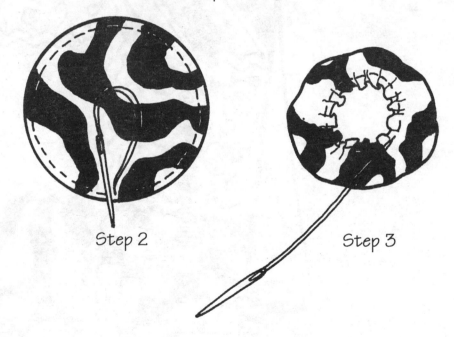

Step 2   Step 3

MORE IDEAS

- Create Yo-Yo flowers of all different sizes.
- Glue buttons to the centers of the flowers.
- Use flowers to decorate a hat, shirt, pair of shoes, quilt squares (see page 103), or the edge of your pillowcase.

Patchwork Picture Frame

Use This Fabulous Fabric Frame for Your Favorite Photo

Patchwork Picture Frame

MATERIALS

- 2 squares of poster board, 9" x 9" (23 cm x 23 cm)
- 8 assorted fabric squares, 3" x 3" (7.5 cm x 7.5 cm)
- Rickrack or ribbon
- Glue
- Scissors
- Photograph, larger than 3" x 5" (7.5 cm x 13 cm)
- Pencil
- Ruler

LET'S DO IT!!

1. Pencil a grid of 3" (7.5 cm) squares on one piece of poster board.
2. Cut the center square out of the grid, creating a picture frame.
3. Glue the fabric squares to the poster board frame. Cover all the edges of the fabric squares with rickrack.
4. Glue the sides and bottom of the frame to the other piece of poster board.
5. Insert your favorite photo into the open top edge, facing out. Position it in place, and glue the top edge of the photo to the inside front of the frame.

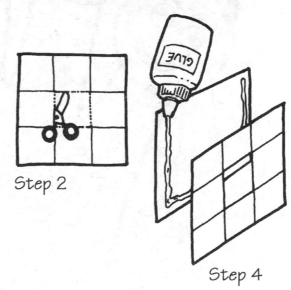

Step 2

Step 4

MORE IDEAS

- Frame a favorite drawing.
- Decorate the frame with buttons or Yo-Yo flowers (see page 109).
- Instead of covering the grids with fabric, color each square of the poster-board grid in a different design.

Puppet Glove

Turn an Old Fabric or Rubber Glove into a Storytelling Prop

Puppet Glove

- Glove
- Felt
- Wiggly eyes
- Yarn
- Pipe cleaners
- Glue
- Scissors

1. Cut out five felt circles about 1" (2.5 cm) in diameter.
2. Glue on wiggly eyes, yarn, and pipe cleaner pieces to create facial features and hair.
3. Glue one face to each finger of the glove.
4. Have a puppet show!

Step 2

Step 3

MORE IDEAS

- Create characters from your favorite fairy tale and act out the story.
- Instead of gluing the faces to the glove fingers, attach them with Velcro so you can add and remove them.
- Cut the fingers off the glove to make individual finger puppets.

Felt Cone Hat

Make and Decorate Hats for a Play or a Party

Felt Cone Hat

- Sheets of felt
- Stapler
- Glue
- Scissors
- Thin elastic

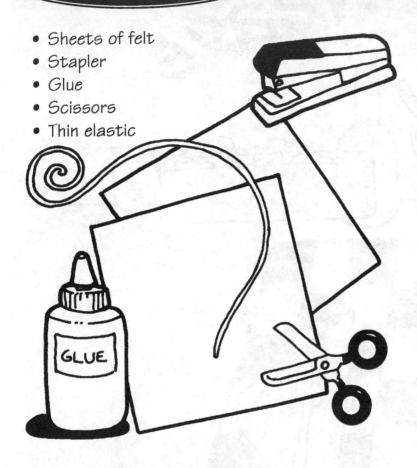

1. Form a cone shape from felt, glue and staple the seam to form a cone hat.
2. Cut a small hole on each side of the hat near the bottom edge.
3. Tie the ends of a length of elastic through the holes to create a chin strap.
4. Glue felt cutouts to the hat to decorate it.

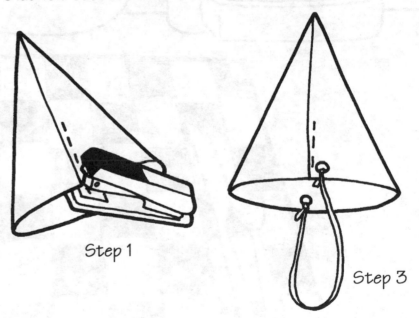

Step 1

Step 3

MORE IDEAS

- Use ribbon for the chin strap and decorate the hat with fabric, yarn, or rickrack.
- Make a Robin Hood or Peter Pan cap. Staple the green felt into a small cone shape and attach a red feather to the side of the hat.
- Braid metallic gold pipe cleaners into a wreath for your cone hat. Attach long pieces of curled ribbon to the back of the wreath.

Stain and Weave

Common Kitchen Dyes Create Colorful Weavings

Stain and Weave

- Muslin fabric, torn into 1" x 12" (2.5 cm x 30 cm) strips
- Cardboard square, 12" x 12" (30.5 cm x 30.5 cm)
- Stapler
- Scissors
- Household dyes: ketchup, spaghetti sauce, chocolate syrup, grape juice, mustard—Anything that will stain!

1. Stain each fabric strip with household dyes.
2. Rinse the strips thoroughly and let them dry.
3. Cover the cardboard with stained strips, laying them side by side.
4. Staple both ends of each strip to the cardboard.
5. Weave the remaining stained strips under and over the stapled strips. Staple the ends of the woven strips to the cardboard.

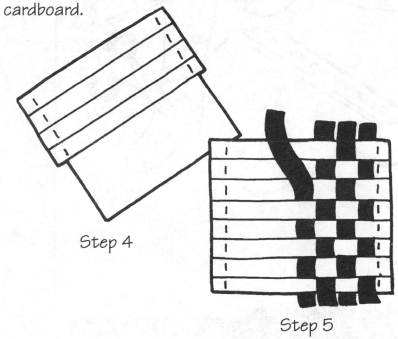

Step 4

Step 5

MORE IDEAS

- Pin the strips to cardboard, weave, remove the pins, and sew the weaving onto a piece of fabric to make a place mat.
- Weave ribbons or different print fabric strips.
- Weave long, flat leaves, such as iris, day lily, or cattail leaves.

Indoor Tennis Racket

- Old nylon stocking
- Wire coat hanger
- Masking tape
- Scissors
- Aluminum foil

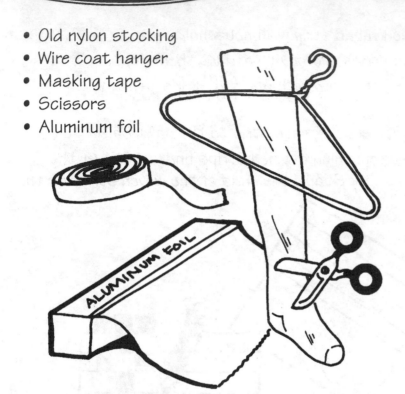

1. Bend the shoulders of the hanger into an oval-shaped frame. Straighten the hook to form a wire handle.
2. Pull a nylon stocking over the oval frame.
3. Cut off the excess stocking that hangs below the end of the handle.
4. Wrap masking tape around and around the stocking and the wire handle to form a padded handle.
5. Make a ball out of aluminum foil and bounce it on your racket.

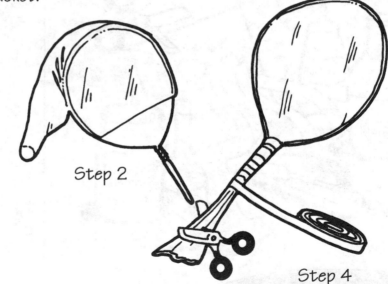

Step 2

Step 4

MORE IDEAS

- Make two rackets and play indoor tennis.
- Play racket basketball by batting a foil ball into a clothes basket. Compete with a friend to see who scores the most baskets.
- Compete with yourself to see how many times you can bounce the ball without letting it fall to the floor.

Pocket Pouch

- Pair of old jeans
- 25" (63.5 cm) piece of ribbon or yarn
- Needle
- Thread
- Scissors

1. Make a pouch by cutting a back pocket out of (not off of) the jeans, leaving the jean material behind the pocket.

2. Sew the ribbon ends to the sides of the pouch to create a carrying strap.

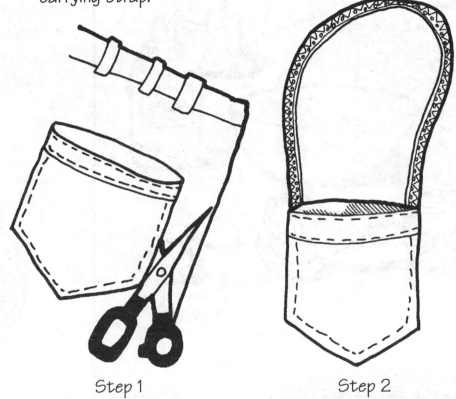

Step 1   Step 2

MORE IDEAS

- Decorate the pouch with lace, sequins, or buttons.
- Cut two slits in the back of the pouch and slide it onto your belt.
- Cut slits all the way around the top of the pouch about one inch apart. Weave the ribbon through the slits to create a drawstring bag.

Yarn Balloon

- Small balloon
- Yarn
- Liquid starch
- Glue
- Bowl
- Fishing line or thread

1. Blow up and tie off the balloon.
2. Mix equal parts of starch and glue in a bowl.
3. Dip pieces of yarn in the mixture and wrap them around the balloon. Let the yarn dry thoroughly.
4. Pop the inside balloon and carefully pull it out of the yarn balloon.
5. Use fishing line or thread to hang the balloon from your ceiling.

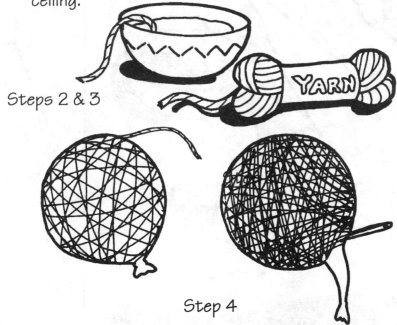

Steps 2 & 3

Step 4

MORE IDEAS

- Use several different colors of yarn to cover the balloon.
- Apply squares of tissue paper to the balloon before winding it with yarn.
- Make a giant Easter egg. Cut a hole in the side of a yarn balloon and fill it with Easter grass and goodies.

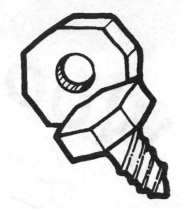

Hardware Handiwork

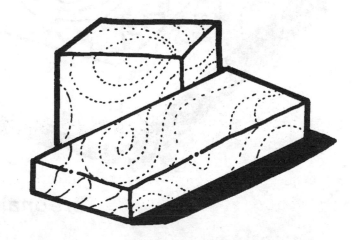

Wooden Nameplate

Personalize This Woodworking Project

Wooden Nameplate

- Flat piece of wood
- Screwdriver
- Hammer or mallet
- Pencil
- Paints
- Paintbrush
- Sandpaper

1. Draw a design around the edges of the piece of wood.
2. Write your name to fill the middle of the piece of wood.
3. With a hammer, tap the blade of a screwdriver into the wood, following the lines of the design and letters.
4. Sand the top and edges of the nameplate so they're smooth.
5. Paint the nameplate to highlight the imprinted design and your name.

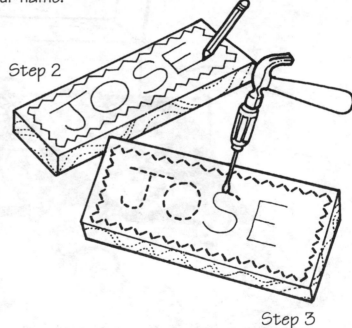

Step 2

Step 3

MORE IDEAS

- Punch and paint a picture into the wood.
- Punch a message, saying, or poem into the wood.
- Use the imprinted and painted piece as a paperweight.

Hardware Jewelry

Jingle and Jangle Wherever You Go!

Hardware Jewelry

- Assorted washers, nuts, or other hardware with a hole in it
- Acrylic paints
- Paintbrush
- Yarn or ribbon
- Wax paper

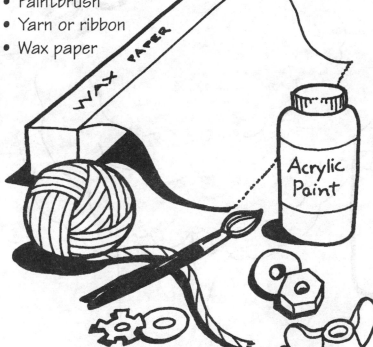

1. Cover your work space with wax paper. Paint your hardware pieces.
2. Let the pieces dry thoroughly on the wax paper.
3. Thread the hardware jewels onto yarn or ribbon and knot between jewels. Tie the ends together, and wear it as a necklace or bracelet.

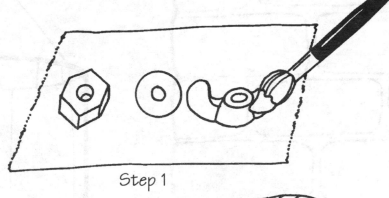

Step 1

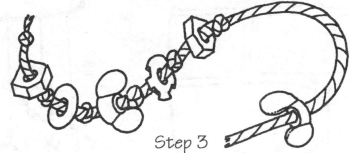

Step 3

MORE IDEAS

- Make a matched set: a necklace, a bracelet, a pin, and earrings. Use jewelry hardware for the earrings and pin.
- Tie painted bolts onto the yarn in between the threaded hardware.
- Thread or sew bells between the hardware.

Metallic Wind Chimes

Hear Your Handiwork Whenever the Wind Blows

Metallic Wind Chimes

- Can opener
- Small can
- Fishing line or strong thread
- Assorted nuts, bolts, washers, or other hardware
- Acrylic paints
- Paintbrush

1. Remove the top, bottom, and label from the can.
2. Wash the can thoroughly and let it dry.
3. Paint the can and the hardware and let them dry.
4. Cut several pieces of fishing line three times as long as the can. Tie one end of the line to a hardware piece and the other end around the can sides, as shown below.
5. Cut three pieces of fishing line about 12" (30 cm) long. Tie one end of each piece to the can and tie the other ends together to create a hanger.

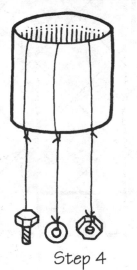

Step 4

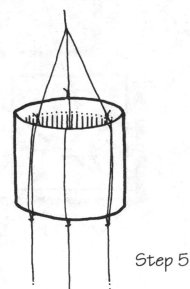

Step 5

MORE IDEAS

- Use nuts or seed pods instead of hardware for a different look and a different sound.
- Curl long lengths of ribbon and hang them from the can.
- Hang some craft sticks with the chimes to help catch the wind.

String Star

Make a Constellation of Pretty Stars

String Star

- Hammer
- Nails
- Pencil
- Wood square
- Colored string or embroidery thread

1. Lightly draw a star on the piece of wood. Along the star outline, mark dots about 1" (2.5 cm) apart.

2. Hammer nails halfway into the wood at the dots.

3. Weave string or thread in and out of the nails and tie them off.

4. Repeat the weaving with different colors until the nails are filled.

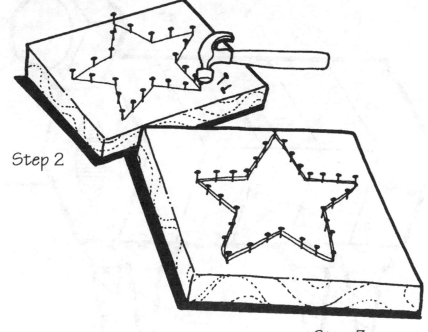

Step 2

Step 3

MORE IDEAS

- Paint the block of wood first. Use yarn or ribbon for weaving.
- Create different shapes such as a heart, a diamond, a butterfly, or a flower.
- Make many stars and hang them in a constellation on your wall.

Bolt Buffalo

Make an Iron Buffalo

Bolt Buffalo

- Assorted hardware such as nuts, screws, washers, wing nuts, and bolts
- Hot-glue gun

LET'S DO IT!!

1. To make the body, glue five of the same-sized nuts in a stack and let them dry.
2. For the head, glue two nuts in a stack and let them dry.
3. Glue the heads of four screws or bolts to the body to create legs.
4. Glue the head to the body.
5. Glue a wing nut to the top of the head to form horns.

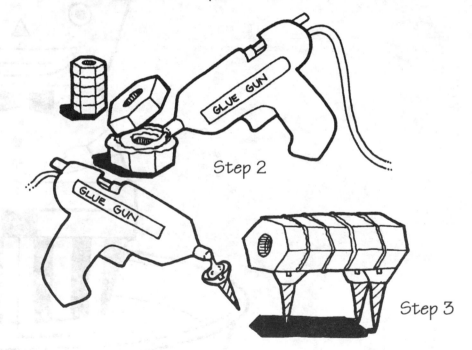

Step 2

Step 3

MORE IDEAS

- Paint your buffalo with acrylic paints.
- Create an entire herd of buffalo.
- Make different animals, people, or aliens.

Flower Pot Clown

Let This Happy Fellow Greet Your Visitors

Flower Pot Clown

- 4 small clay pots
- Clay saucer
- Hot-glue gun
- Acrylic paints
- Paintbrush

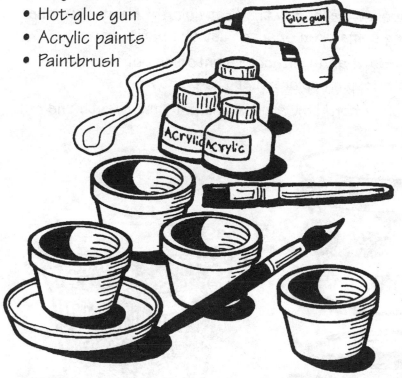

1. Glue two of the pots rim to rim, and then do the same with the other two pots.
2. Glue the sets together end to end to create a stack of four pots.
3. Glue the saucer to one end of the stack.
4. Paint a clown: the top pot as hat or hair, the second pot as a face, the third pot as a shirt, and the fourth pot as pants.

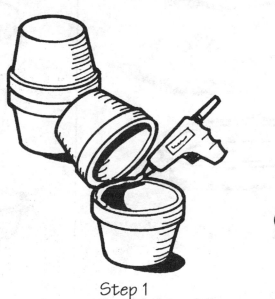

Step 1

Step 3

MORE IDEAS

- Add construction paper or cardboard hands and feet.
- Decorate the clown with fabric and yarn scraps.
- Paint the pots to look like a character from your favorite book or cartoon.
- Use the character as a decoration in your house or outdoors.

Sponge Painted Pot

- Small clay pot
- Acrylic paints
- Sponge
- Pie tins
- Ribbon or cord

1. Squirt blobs of the paints into pie tins.
2. Cut a sponge into small pieces, about 1" (2.5 cm) square.
3. Using a sponge piece, dab the first color of paint onto the pot, leaving some open spaces. Let the paint dry.
4. Dab the second and third colors onto the pot and in the spaces, overlapping colors. Let the paint dry.
5. Tie a ribbon or cord bow around the pot underneath the rim.

Step 3

Step 5

MORE IDEAS

- Use metallic gold paint to give your pot an elegant touch. Tie on gold cord.
- Use the pot as a Mother's Day gift or as a gift for a teacher. Plant a real plant in it or fill the pot with pretty silk flowers.
- Cut out shapes and use a sponge to stencil them onto the pots.

Clay Pot Votive Candle

MATERIALS

- Small clay pot
- Paraffin
- Coffee can
- Hot pads or mitts
- Candle wicking or string
- Saucepan
- Aluminum foil
- Craft stick

MORE IDEAS

LET'S DO IT!!

1. Tie a length of wicking to the center of a craft stick.
2. Place some paraffin in a coffee can and place the can in a saucepan of boiling water to melt the paraffin.
3. Place a piece of aluminum foil in the clay pot to cover the drainage hole.
4. Pour the melted paraffin into the clay pot. Be careful not to burn your hands on the hot coffee can. Use mitts or ask an adult to help you with this part.
5. Lower the wicking into the center of the paraffin, resting the craft stick on the rim of the pot. Let the paraffin cool and harden and then clip the craft stick off, leaving a wick.

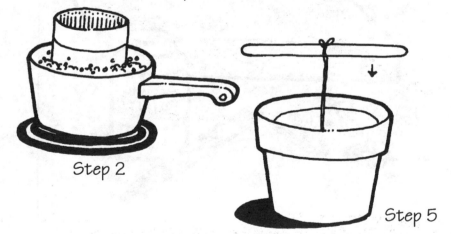

Step 2

Step 5

- Add potpourri oil (available at craft stores) to the paraffin for scented candles.
- Add crushed herbs to the paraffin. When the paraffin is dry, coat the rim of the pot with glue, and then dip the rim in crushed herbs.
- Decorate the pot with acrylic paints, using a paintbrush or the sponge method (see page 134).

Cup Hook Key Holder

- Wooden rectangle
- 3 cup hooks
- Pencil
- Ruler
- Acrylic paints
- Paintbrush or sponges
- Hot-glue gun
- Paper clip

1. On the piece of wood, mark three dots spaced equally apart.
2. Screw the cup hooks into the wood at the dots.
3. Glue a paper clip to the back of the wood for a hanger.
4. Decorate the key holder with paint.
5. Hang the key holder in a handy place in your home.

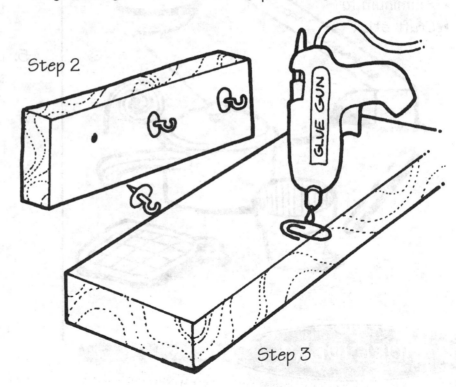

Step 2

Step 3

MORE IDEAS

- With a hammer and nail, tap a small hole at each dot to make it easier to screw in the cup hooks.
- Paint a message over the hooks, such as "Keys to My Heart" or "Dad's Keys."
- Decorate the key holder with sequins and glitter.

Junk Sculpture

- Cardboard
- Scissors
- Glue
- Assorted junk

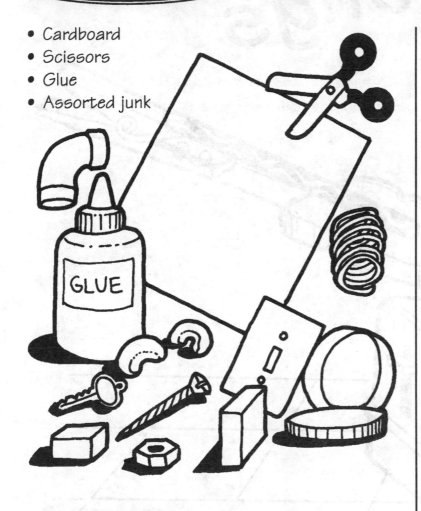

1. Cut a cardboard base large enough to accommodate your sculpture.
2. Gather together junk pieces such as jar lids, packing peanuts, old keys, scrap wood, nuts, bolts, screws, springs, and parts from broken appliances.
3. Glue the junk pieces to the cardboard and to each other, creating an interesting three-dimensional sculpture.

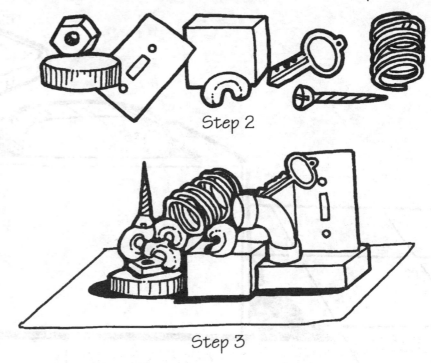

Step 2

Step 3

MORE IDEAS

- Build something realistic with your junk pieces.
- Collect items from nature to add to your sculpture.
- Paint the cardboard base and the junk pieces different colors before you create your artwork.

Toast Tongs

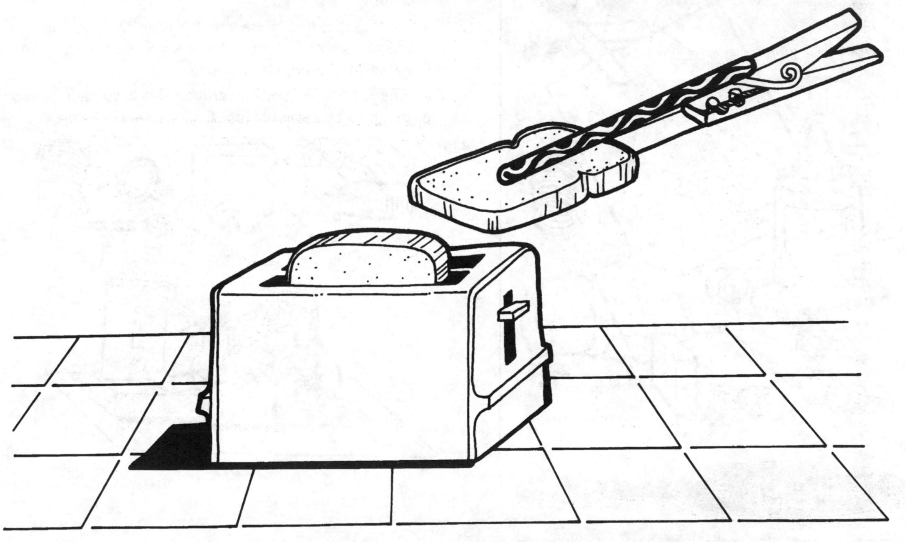

No More Toasted Fingers in the Mornings

Toast Tongs

- Wooden spring clothespin
- Two large craft sticks
- Glue
- Acrylic paints
- Paintbrush

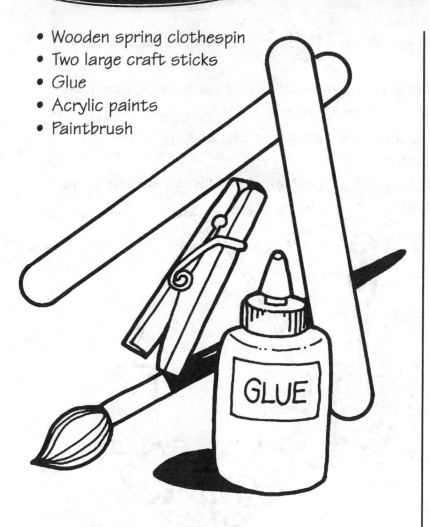

LET'S DO IT!!

1. Glue the end of one craft stick to the clothespin just below the spring and let it dry.

2. Glue the second craft stick to the other side of the clothespin and let it dry.

3. Paint the tongs on the outside only.

4. Use them to pull hot toast out of the toaster.

Step 1

Step 3

MORE IDEAS

- Write a message on the tongs or personalize them with a name.
- Give tongs as a gift along with a sugar-and-cinnamon shaker and a loaf of homemade bread.

Pumice Necklace

- Pumice stone
- Table knife
- Screwdriver, ice pick, or metal knitting needle
- Leather thong or string

1. Cut the pumice into 1" (2.5 cm) blocks, using the table knife.
2. Bore a hole through the middle of each block, using a screwdriver, ice pick, or knitting needle.
3. Cut a leather thong or string long enough to fit over your head.
4. String the pumice blocks onto the thong, knotting the ends together.

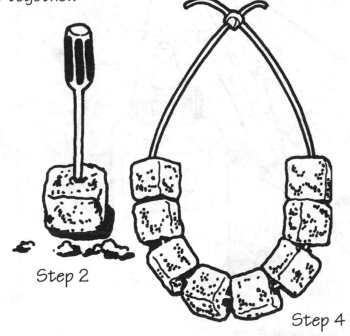

Step 2

Step 4

MORE IDEAS

- Paint the stones with acrylic paints.
- Scrape the pumice blocks on a sidewalk to form rounder beads.
- Wear the necklace in the tub, sink down into the water, and watch your necklace float!

Trash Treasures

Canned Candle

Place Several of These on a Mantle or Use as a Centerpiece

Canned Candle

- 8-ounce (227 g) can, cleaned and dried
- Votive candle
- Acrylic paints
- Paintbrush
- Toothbrush

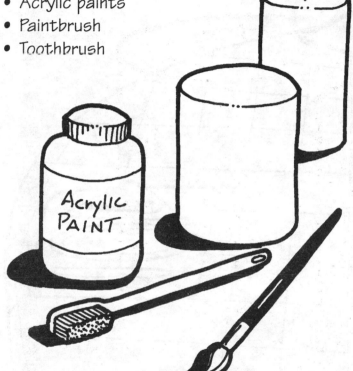

1. Paint the outside of the can a solid color and let it dry.
2. Paint a scene or design on the can.
3. Dip a toothbrush in paint and spatter paint all over the design (see page 17).
4. Place the votive candle in the can.

Step 2   Step 3

MORE IDEAS

- Spatter white paint to look like snow or spatter several colors for a speckled look.
- Clean and dry a larger can, such as a soup can. Fill the can with sand to avoid denting. Then, use a hammer and nail to carefully punch a design in the can. Empty the sand from the can and insert a votive candle.
- Create a variety of sizes of canned candles and display them all together.

Milk Jug Swan

Let This Swan Grace Your Dinner Table

Milk Jug Swan

- 1-gallon (3.8 L) plastic milk jug
- Scissors
- Dishwashing soap
- White tempera paint
- Paintbrush
- Paper napkin
- Glue
- Construction paper

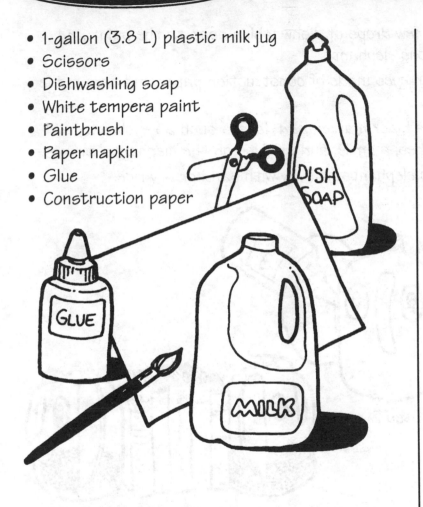

1. Cut off the top half of the jug, making a zigzag cut and leaving the handle intact.
2. Curl the feathers by rolling and bending the points of the zigzags.
3. Add a few drops of dishwashing soap to the paint and paint the swan.
4. To create the head, crumple a napkin into a ball, glue it to the top of the handle, and glue on a construction paper beak and eyes.

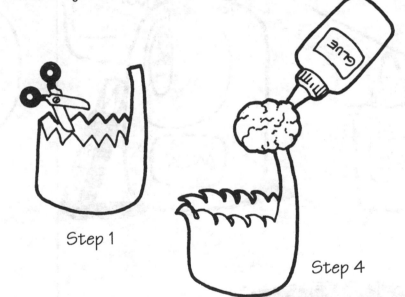

Step 1

Step 4

MORE IDEAS

- Fill the swan with Easter grass and use it as a basket.
- Use the swan as a planter.
- Place a square box of tissues into the swan and use it as a tissue holder.

Elephant Bookends

- Two 1-gallon (3.8 L) plastic milk jugs
- Gray tempera paint
- Dishwashing soap
- Paintbrush
- Gray felt
- Black marker
- Construction paper
- Sand or uncooked rice
- Glue

1. Add a few drops of dishwashing soap to the paint and paint the elephants.
2. Glue on eyes made of construction paper and ears made of felt.
3. Using a black marker, add details such as eyebrows, eyelashes, a smile, and wrinkles on the elephants' trunks.
4. Fill the elephants halfway with sand or dry rice.

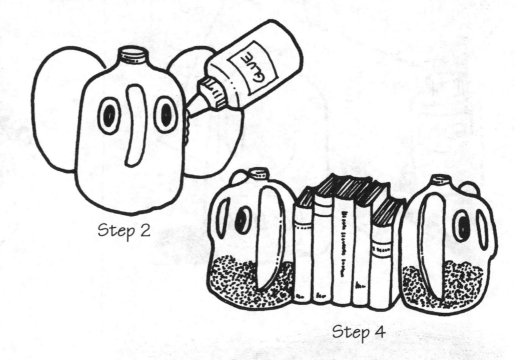

Step 2

Step 4

MORE IDEAS

- Use an elephant as a doorstop.
- Make different kinds of animals.
- Paint the elephants wild colors and decorate them like circus elephants.

Foam Drink Coasters

- Foam meat trays
- Hole punch
- Ribbon or yarn
- Scissors

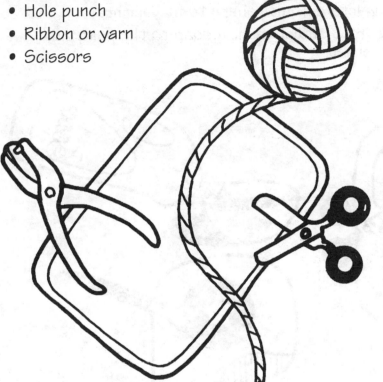

1. Cut the foam trays into 4" (10 cm) circles.
2. Punch holes around the edge of each foam circle.
3. Lace ribbon through the holes and tie the ribbon ends in a bow.

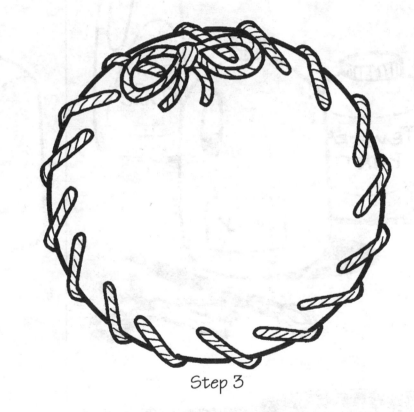

Step 3

MORE IDEAS

- Cut out coasters of different shapes.
- Glue a picture on the center of each coaster and cover it with clear contact paper.
- Personalize the coasters by painting names on them with acrylic paints.

Plastic Helmet

- 1-gallon (3.8 L) plastic milk jug
- Tempera paints
- Paintbrush
- Dishwashing soap
- Scissors

1. Cut the handle and the spout off the jug.
2. Trim the jug into a helmet shape to fit your head.
3. Add a few drops of dishwashing soap to the paint and paint the helmet.

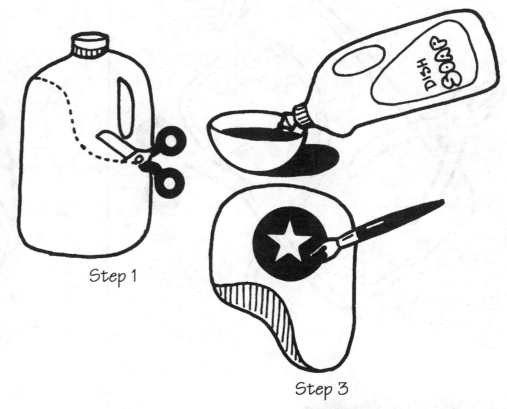

Step 1

Step 3

MORE IDEAS

- Paint the helmet gray and add a topknot of red feathers to make a knight's helmet.
- Paint the helmet with acrylic paints if you decide to wear it as part of a costume.
- Make a helmet for each of your favorite teams.

Egg Carton Characters

- Egg carton
- Fabric, buttons, pipe cleaners, glitter, and sequins
- Scissors
- Markers
- Glue, tape, or stapler

1. Cut the lid from the egg carton and save it.
2. Cut out the individual egg cups to make heads.
3. Add facial features to the characters by gluing on fabric, buttons, glitter, and sequins.
4. Set the characters on the lid to dry and to display.

Step 4

MORE IDEAS

- Stack several cups to make a tall character.
- Make animals, aliens, family members, or storybook characters.
- Create flowers by painting the cups and adding pipe cleaner stems.

Juice Can Junk Holder

- Juice can—empty, clean, and dry
- Masking tape
- Brown shoe polish
- Paper towels

1. Cover the outside of the can with overlapping short strips of masking tape.
2. Use paper towels to rub shoe polish onto the sides of the can to give it an antique look.
3. Wipe off the excess shoe polish and let the can dry.

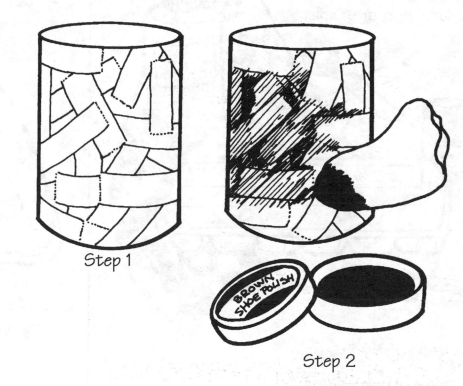

Step 1

Step 2

MORE IDEAS

- Use other colors of shoe polish and different sizes of cans for different effects.
- Use as a vase for artificial flowers or tissue flowers (see page 15).
- Glue glitter, sequins, or items found in nature to the sides of the can to decorate it.

Egg Carton Sailboat

- Foam egg carton
- Clay
- Toothpick
- Tape
- Paper
- Crayons or markers
- Scissors

1. Cut out an individual egg cup.
2. Press a small ball of play clay into the bottom of the egg cup.
3. Cut out and decorate a paper triangle about as high and wide as the egg cup.
4. Tape one end of the toothpick to the center of the paper triangle.
5. Stick the other end of the toothpick into the clay ball and float the sailboat in a tub of cold water.

Step 4

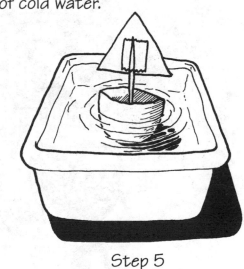

Step 5

MORE IDEAS

- Use the remaining egg cups to create an entire fleet of sailboats.
- Cut a boat shape from a foam meat tray. Make a paper sail as described in the directions but insert the toothpick directly into the foam tray.
- Hold sailboat races. See who can blow his or her sailboat to the end of the tub first. See which boat design sails faster—the egg cup or the foam tray.

Six-Pack-Ring Weaving

Make an Interesting and Colorful Wall Hanging

Six-Pack-Ring Weaving

- 4 plastic six-pack rings
- Twist ties
- Yarn, string, and ribbon
- Strips of paper or fabric
- Glue
- Scissors

1. Attach the rings together with twist ties to form a large rectangle.

2. Weave yarn, string, ribbon, and paper or fabric strips through the holes.

3. Trim the excess weaving materials around the edges and glue the ends to the plastic rings.

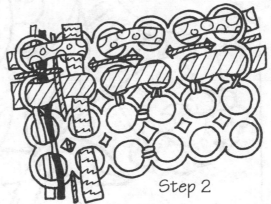

Step 2

Step 3

MORE IDEAS

- Make a larger weaving by using more six-pack rings.
- Weave in items collected from nature.
- Weave a set of place mats.

Styrofoam Cup Daffodils

Create a Beautiful Handmade Bouquet

Styrofoam Cup Daffodils

- Styrofoam cup
- Egg carton cup
- Glue
- Green pipe cleaner
- Green construction paper
- Orange and yellow tempera paint
- Paintbrush

1. Cut points around the edge of the foam cup and place it in a warm oven (200° F/94° C) for a few minutes to let the points curl.

2. Paint the cup yellow. Paint an egg carton cup orange.

3. Glue the egg carton cup inside the foam cup.

4. Glue the blossom to a pipe cleaner. Glue on leaves.

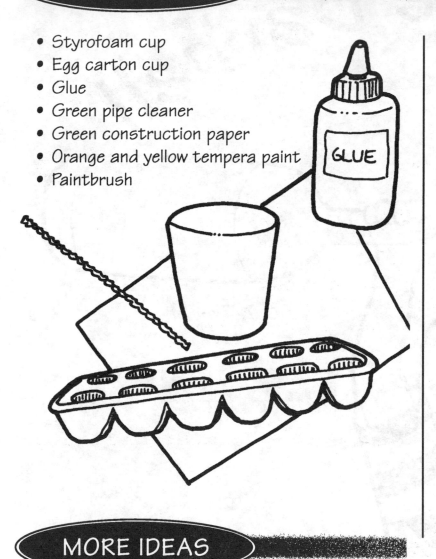

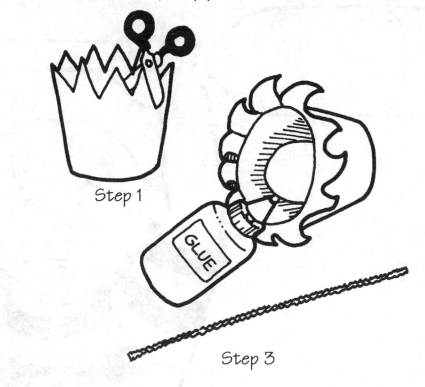

Step 1

Step 3

MORE IDEAS

- Watch the cooking step carefully. If the cup is left in the oven too long, the Styrofoam will melt.
- Make a mixed bouquet. Paint flowers of different colors. Combine them with tissue flowers (see page 15).
- Use small wads of colored tissue paper as centers and glue them in the flower cups.

Soda Bottle Barbell

Get a Good Workout at Home

Soda Bottle Barbell

- Two 2-liter soda bottles
- 3' (0.91 m) of ¾" (2 cm) plastic pipe
- Duct tape
- Sand or dry rice

RICE

1. Discard the soda bottle caps.
2. Fill the bottles halfway with sand or rice.
3. Insert one end of the pipe into the neck of one bottle and the other end of the pipe into the other bottle.
4. Seal the pipe to the bottles with duct tape.

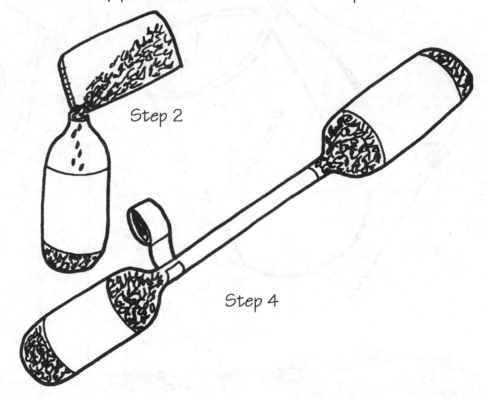

Step 2

Step 4

MORE IDEAS

- Leave the bottles empty and use the barbell as a balancing stick for pretend tightrope walking.
- Use smaller soda bottles and shorter pipe to make individual hand weights.
- Attach one empty bottle and use it as a bat with an aluminum foil ball.

Crushed Can Critter

- Can—empty, clean, and dry
- Paper or felt
- Pipe cleaners
- Wiggly eyes

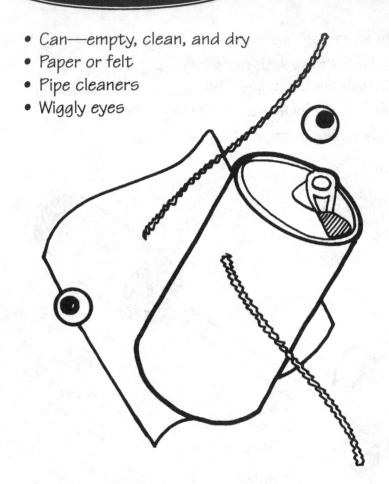

1. Crush the can by stomping on it.
2. Using the drink hole as the mouth, add wiggly eyes, and use paper, felt, and pipe cleaners to add facial features.

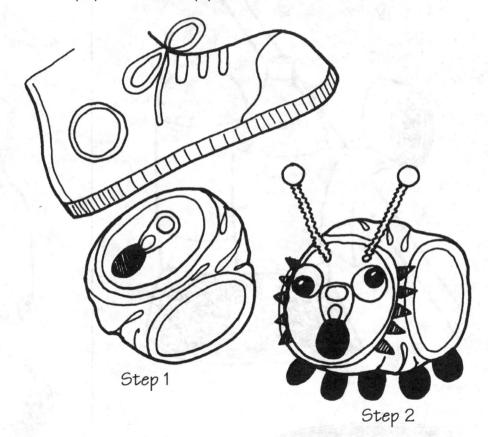

Step 1

Step 2

MORE IDEAS

- Create a mobile by making several critters. Punch a hole in each one and hang them with string from a coat hanger.
- Use the critters to create a wind chime.
- Decorate a set of critters the same and use them as game pieces on an outdoor tic-tac-toe game board (see page 66.)

Index

Index (cont.)